KNOCK AND THE DOOR WILL OPEN

ALSO BY JEFFREY A. WANDS

Another Door Opens

The Psychic in You

KNOCK AND THE DOOR WILL OPEN

6 Keys to Mastering the Art of Living

JEFFREY A. WANDS

ATRIA PAPERBACK

New York   London   Toronto   Sydney

ATRIA PAPERBACK

A Division of Simon & Schuster, Inc.
1230 Avenue of the Americas
New York, NY 10020

First Atria Paperback edition June 2010

ATRIA PAPERBACK and colophon are trademarks of Simon & Schuster, Inc.

For information about special discounts for bulk purchases, please contact
Simon & Schuster Special Sales at 1-866-506-1949 or business@simonandschuster.com.

The Simon & Schuster Speakers Bureau can bring authors to your live event.
For more information or to book an event contact the Simon & Schuster
Speakers Bureau at 1-866-248-3049 or visit our website at www.simonspeakers.com.

Designed by Joel Avirom and Jason Snyder

Manufactured in the United States of America

10   9   8   7   6   5   4   3   2

Library of Congress Cataloging-in-Publication Data is available

ISBN 978-1-4165-9108-5
ISBN 978-1-4165-9749-0 (ebook)

As always, my deepest and most heartfelt thanks to my wife,
Dawn, and our boys, Christopher and Robert, as well as to all those
I have encountered on this, my journey of love and life!

ACKNOWLEDGMENTS

Thanks to my clients for your trust and for reminding me every day of my life purpose. Thank you all my friends at WALK-FM radio, *The Breakfast Club with Mark and Cindy*, and to all the listeners who have called during my program and attended my shows. To Judy Kern, who helped with every step of the writing of this book, and to my agents, Liv and Bill Blumer. To my editor, Johanna Castillo, and to all the wonderful, supportive people at Atria, especially Carolyn Reidy and Judith Curr. Special thanks to Judy Martin for your expertise in work/ life. With gratitude to my wonderful assistant, Theresa O'Kelly-Moriarty, for always showing me your support and for being my trusted right hand. To the *Maury* show and its terrific staff who always strive to make each of my appearances better than the last; with special thanks to Paul Faulhaber, Joan Petrocelli-Doumas, Morgan Landau, as well as the infamous John Pascarella. Finally, to everyone else who has contributed to and made this experience so very special for me!

CONTENTS

RECOGNIZE THE TREASURES YOU'VE BEEN GIVEN AND THOSE THAT ARE OUT THERE FOR YOU

I'm a psychic and a medium, which means it is both my calling and my work not only to connect people on the physical plane with loved ones in the world of spirit but also to help my clients discover why their lives might not be as rich and fulfilling as they had hoped, and sometimes to help them make the changes that will lead them down a different, more rewarding path.

It took me a long time before I was able to acknowledge my psychic gift as something to be treasured. I didn't accept what I'd been given as a blessing. Like many people, I was allowing my fears to get in the way of my success. I was afraid of being seen as different or even weird. I thought people might be afraid to talk to me because they'd

1

think I was reading their minds. Over the years, however, I've come to understand that my psychic abilities allow me to help people improve their lives; once I was able to embrace that truth, my own life became richer and more meaningful as well. What I've learned in the course of my own journey and now want to share with you is that life for every one of us is like a giant treasure chest just waiting to be filled with all the gifts we've been given and the new treasures that are out there for us to collect, if only we are willing to embark on an exciting, if sometimes scary, journey of discovery.

Why scary? Because like any journey into uncharted territory, it takes us out of our comfort zone. It's just easier for most of us to cling to what's familiar, even if it isn't making us happy. We live in a society that has conditioned us to expect the worst instead of the best. Turn on your television or pick up the paper any day of the week and you're sure to be bombarded with messages of gloom and doom. From the weather to the economy, the media know that bad news sells. And once all that bad news takes up residence in our subconscious minds, it's what we come to believe. As a result, we all tend to operate from a place of fear—especially fear of change.

If there's anything I've learned as a psychic, however, it's that the mind is a powerful tool. Whatever we can conceive with our minds we can manifest in our lives. Change your mind and you can change your life. The key is to let go of the fear that may be keeping you stuck in a rut, believe that it's possible to change, and then empower yourself to make it happen.

In times past, psychics were sometimes called "intuitives." Another old word for psychic is "clairvoyant," meaning "one who sees clearly." In truth, however, we are all born with intuition and the ability to see clearly. We all have the capacity to focus our energy and tune into what's working or not working for us, figure out why, and then make the adjustments that will help us create more positive results in the future.

To help you learn how to do this, I suggest that you think about it in terms of electrical energy. We put a plug in a socket and the light or the television or the computer springs to life. But that energy is always out there, whether we're plugged into it or not. Ironically, the more plugged in we've become, the more disconnected we are from the invisible energy that's within and all around us. Your thoughts, like everything else in the universe, have energy. What you need to do is plug in the radio of your mind and tune it to the right frequency. What I'm going to be doing in this book is help you to reconnect with your own psychic energy so that you can begin to make the most of the valuable gifts you've been given and attract the many treasures that are out there for the taking.

Of course, if you think of your life as a treasure chest, you must realize that there is only so much room available. Therefore, to fill it with what is truly valuable, you will probably need to discard some of the fool's gold you've been hoarding. That means letting go of old fears, anger, grievances, or misconceptions that may have been taking up space in your mind so that you can make room for the new beliefs about yourself and the universe that will take you to new levels of peace and achievement of purpose.

In my first book, *The Psychic in You*, I helped people tap into their ability to connect with those in the world of spirit. In this book I'm going to help you connect more deeply with yourself. I often tell people that our present is governed by our past and that we need to get in touch with the past and then shift our conscious and unconscious beliefs about it so we can act differently now and create a better future for ourselves.

✦ ✦ ✦

I believe that there are six basic keys to unlocking life's treasures, the first of which is to examine yourself and, with honesty and clarity, determine what it is about yourself and your life that makes you happy right now and what it is you would like to get rid of or improve. Grabbing hold of that key and putting it in the lock might take some courage, because you might be reluctant to look too closely at the potentially toxic stuff you've been storing in the attic of your mind. But it's going to be worth it, because once you've brought all that stuff out into the daylight and let it go, you'll feel lighter and freer and better able to begin the rest of your journey of discovery.

After doing the self-examination, there are five more keys—important areas we all need to work on in order to make our lives better.

The second key is to examine all of our relationships—those with people who are in our daily lives right now as well as with those with people who have passed on to the world of spirit. We all have relationships we need to treasure as well as those that fill us with negativity and self-doubt. I'll be helping you not only to figure out which is which but also to let go of the ones that are keeping you from thriving.

The third key is to make certain that your actual physical environment—your home and your place of work—are really working for you. The ancient Chinese understood very well how every aspect of your physical space can affect your health and well-being. You may not have thought that a physical space has energy, but it does. In this section we'll be looking at how you can use a bit of psychic feng shui to change that energy and create an environment that enhances your peace and prosperity and maximizes the flow of positive energy in your life.

The fourth key area we need to think about is how to bring more prosperity into our lives. On some level, of course, this means increasing material wealth. But there's more to prosperity than money. As I hope to make you understand, discovering your true path and following your passion will be not only the surest but also the most fulfilling way to increase your wealth and well-being.

The fifth key is to increase your spiritual strength. Some of you may already be affiliated with an organized religious community. But spirituality does not require you to follow any particular belief system or attend a particular house of worship. All that's required is for you to find a way to affirm your belief in a higher power—however you choose to conceive of and envision that power—which will help you to internalize your faith that whatever comes into your life happens for a purpose. As you'll discover, we are all born with spirituality; we just need to believe in it, treasure it, and work at developing what we've been given.

And, finally, the sixth key is to achieve the balance we all seek in our lives by ensuring that we nourish our emotional and physical well-being. The mind and body have powerful effects on each other; what strengthens one also benefits the other, and when one suffers they both feel the pain. The key here is to control your emotions and take care of your body. Not only will I be helping you understand that you have the power to take charge of your emotions, I will also be helping you develop the tools you need to do it. And I'll be showing you how and why taking care of your physical health will positively impact your mental outlook.

To help you remain focused and increase your understanding as you explore these six keys, you'll find brief aphorisms marked "A Word to the Wise" placed throughout the book. I hope you'll use these words to inspire you and affirm your intentions.

✦ ✦ ✦

Some locks are stickier than others; sometimes it's harder to turn the key and open the door to discovery. There are treasures behind all these doors, so if one is stubbornly refusing to yield, please do whatever it takes to unlock it.

One thing I've learned is that there are many ways to achieve a particular goal. As you'll see, I've taken what I can from a variety of philosophies and belief systems. You may be more comfortable with one suggestion or method than another, and that's okay. I just urge you to keep an open mind and not reject any possibility simply because it's new or unfamiliar.

I invite you to open yourself up, look at every aspect of your life, and use all the tools I'll be giving you to discover your personal treasures and make your life as valuable as it can be.

EVALUATE YOURSELF

Before we begin to make changes, we need to be clear about what we want to change and, most importantly, what we want to bring into our lives.

As I've already said, your life is a treasure chest of possibilities just waiting to be filled. What you choose to fill it with is up to you, but you'll want to be sure that you're making good choices so that all your treasures have real worth. What you surely don't want is to spend a lot of time collecting trinkets that take up a great deal of space in your life without providing any real value.

Confront the dark parts of yourself, and work to banish them with illumination and forgiveness. Your willingness to wrestle with your demons will cause your angels to sing.

—August Wilson

Do you remember those arcade games where you put a quarter in the slot and tried to maneuver a claw on a chain to pick up a particular prize? You had to direct the claw to grasp the prize you valued and avoid the ones you didn't want. Well, in many ways, life can be like that game.

In the game of life, you want to be certain that the treasures you store in your chest have value for you. To do that, you first need to make an honest assessment of yourself. I know from long experience that being honest takes courage and a desire for change, so the first step is to get rid of any negativity you may be harboring about this process and relinquish your fears. Intention can be the greatest gift in your life. Thoughts can be as destructive as a killer weed or as productive as a potent fertilizer.

The biggest problem many of us have reaching our goals is that we get in our own way and trip ourselves up. Psychologically and physically we humans are hard-wired to avoid change. Homeostasis, or internal stability, is the condition our bodies seek to maintain at all times. That means keeping our body temperature, heartbeat, blood sugar, and other internal systems working at the optimum level. Normally, we don't think about these things; they just happen automatically. It's only when one of our systems goes awry, when we're not feeling well, that we begin to think about them at all.

That's all well and good where our bodily systems are concerned, but psychologically and emotionally we also tend to avoid change, and that's where we create problems for ourselves. We need to keep in mind that there is no growth without change. To the extent that we continue harboring doubts and fears about ourselves and our abilities, we are preventing ourselves from using our gifts to create the changes that will make our lives more fulfilling.

That's not to say that there won't be rough spots ahead. Just remember that sometimes the experiences that initially cause us the most pain turn out to be the most positive. Having the courage to go through the pain that sometimes accompanies significant change can create life-enhancing breakthrough moments. I often tell my clients to compare it to the experience of childbirth: it's painful, certainly, but also monumentally joyous.

Give Yourself an Emotional Checkup

If you thought there was something physically wrong with you, you'd probably schedule an appointment with your doctor. But it's also important to make an appointment with yourself for an emotional checkup:

- ➤ Are you angry? With whom? Why?

- ➤ Are you disappointed? With yourself? With someone in your life? With your career? With your personal life?

- ➤ Are you worried? About what? Finances? Health? Social life? Sex life? Your career?

There's nothing wrong with experiencing any of these emotions.

We all experience all kinds of emotions all the time. But if you discover that you're hanging on to negative or painful emotions that are making you miserable, you need to get to the source so that you can figure out how to release them. We're all very good at holding on to negative emotions and complaining about our lives. But that's just wasting energy.

If your problem were physical, you'd do something about curing it. So think about what you can do to cure your emotional problem. Really sit down and think about what you can do right now to shift those negative emotions—and then *do it*. You have to live what you believe; don't just tell yourself that you'll get to it when you have more time. Take care of it now—as you would if you were in physical pain.

--------- *A Word to the Wise* ---------

Your emotional life is constantly under construction; make a punch list of items you need to improve and start crossing them off as you accomplish them.

Don't do this just once and think that you're done with it. Take your emotional temperature from time to time to see how much progress you've made. The more self-knowledge you have, the more you'll be able to change the things you don't like about yourself or the way your life is going.

Why Are You Afraid?

Fear is universal. It's a basic survival mechanism that occurs in response to pain, and it can override our best instincts when we sense danger. What's important is the way we respond to our fears. On the positive side, examining our fears allows us to gain a better understanding of ourselves. And once we understand where our fear is coming from, we can gain control over it, rather than letting it control us.

On the negative side, if we don't face our fear it can be the most debilitating of all emotions, preventing us from moving forward with our lives. I like to compare fears we don't face to an untreated infection. If we nip it in the bud, the infection will be cured quickly, but if we don't deal with it, it will spread and become harder and harder to cure.

A client came to me in the midst of the economic meltdown of 2008, wanting advice on whether or not to take the opportunity she'd been offered to participate in a new business venture. My client, whom I'll call Amanda, was an outgoing and engaging young woman. She was an event planner, and the new venture was going to help people create successful fun parties on a budget. It seemed like a perfect time to launch this kind of business, but Amanda was too busy looking at the potentially negative outcomes to see the positives. She was so paralyzed by her fear of failing that she was incapable of moving forward.

There is no passion so contagious as that of fear.
—Michel de Montaisne

As I explained to her, life is like a race. If you start the race afraid that you'll fall down or hurt yourself or that you won't be able to finish, all those negative thoughts are going to keep you from running the best race you're capable of.

One of my own biggest fears was speaking to a large group of people, and since I often do events where hundreds of people come to experience my spontaneous readings, that was a big problem for me. My way of confronting and dealing with my fear was to tell myself that the audience was made up of individuals, and I had no problem speaking to individuals. In addition, I reminded myself that each one of these individuals had chosen to come and hear what I had to say. By changing the way I thought about the situation, I was able to get over my fear.

The surest way to sabotage your own success is to let your fears get in the way. Are you afraid to try for what you want because you're afraid you won't get it? Are you afraid to assert yourself? Do you believe that your needs are less important than someone else's (or everyone else's)? Are you afraid that if you do get what you want it won't be as great as you'd thought it would be and that you might be missing out on something even better down the road? Are you afraid to try something new because you might not be good at it? If you insist on perfection in everything you do you'll probably keep putting things off and never do anything at all. If, for instance, you have a great idea for a new business or a new product and you're so afraid of not getting it exactly right that you never do anything to implement your idea, chances are you'll be sitting in your living room and hearing on the six o'clock news about someone who did exactly what it was that you were afraid to try. The flip side of that coin might be that you always assume someone else who is smarter has already thought of whatever idea you come up with, so you never even bother to investigate whether or not it is feasible. Striving for success doesn't always feel safe; you simply need to trust in your own abilities and embrace the process.

I should also point out, however, that living fearlessly is not the same thing as living recklessly. You don't want to live a reckless life; what you want is to live a fulfilling life, which means not allowing your fears to prevent you from achieving all you are capable of.

In my experience what most of us fear most is the unknown. But if you dwell on your fear you'll be preventing yourself from acquiring the knowledge you need to conquer the unfamiliar. The more you explore your new situation, the less unfamiliar it will be and, there-

Each time we face our fear we gain strength, courage, and confidence in the doing.

—Source Unknown

fore, the less you'll have to fear. In addition, each time you conquer a fear and move into the unknown, you're building confidence in your ability to deal with the next unexpected or unfamiliar situation that comes your way—and it will, because life is all about moving forward, learning, and growing.

Do You Create Your Own Fear?

To large degree our fears are projections of our own minds. Let's say, for example, you're sitting on a park bench on a warm spring day reading a book. You're relaxed and content until someone sits down next to you and distracts you. At that point you might begin to wonder who he is, why he's chosen to sit there, whether he has some ulterior motive. Suddenly, for no reason at all, you're afraid of this poor guy who's just trying to enjoy the day the same way you were until he got there. This is what happens with most panic attacks. If you were afraid of riding in an elevator, you'd begin to anticipate what *might* happen once you got into the elevator—it's going to get stuck and I'm going to be in there for hours, and no one's going to get me out—and on and on until you're paralyzed by a fear that is entirely a creation of your own imagination.

Realize deeply that the present moment is all you ever have. Make the Now the primary focus of your life.

—Eckhart Tolle

Winston Churchill once famously said, "For myself, I'm an optimist. It does not seem to be much use being anything else." What Churchill understood that many of us don't is that we can *choose* to look at the glass as half full, we can *choose* to look on the bright side, or we can *choose* to wallow in our own negativity and dark thoughts. It's looking at the bright side of life that will ultimately bring you inner peace.

Why not postpone your worry until something bad really does happen? I don't mean that you should go through life being totally irresponsible and never planning for the future. Just learn to accept the fact that you will never have total control over what hasn't happened yet and may never happen at all so that you can enjoy what's happening right now.

One problem with worrying about what might happen is that very often, it doesn't, and something else does. Then we blame ourselves for having worried about the wrong thing. A woman recently phoned in to my radio program and told me that she couldn't accept her father's death because he hadn't died from what he was supposed to. He'd had various health problems that she'd been worrying about, but he died unexpectedly from a spontaneous brain bleed that no one could have predicted. Somehow this woman thought she should have known. But she couldn't have. All the worrying in the world wouldn't have changed what happened.

A Word to the Wise

As you ride the roller coaster of life, you can choose to see it as invigorating rather than frightening.

The problem for too many of us is that as soon as times are good and we're happy with the way our life is going, we begin to worry about the next bad thing that *might* happen. Negative thoughts create a vicious cycle. Once you start thinking negatively, chances are that your thoughts will start dragging you down into a vortex of further negativity and fear. What happens then is that you start to operate from a position of fear, trying to avoid whatever bad thing you've convinced yourself might happen instead of going forth with the confidence that you can create something good for yourself. You begin to think of yourself as a victim of fate rather than the master of your own fate.

One woman who came to see me was so terrified of flying that she wasn't even going to attend her own son's wedding. She had one of the worst cases of the "what ifs" I've ever encountered. *What if the pilot falls asleep? What if the pilot has a heart attack?* She wasn't even focusing on the things that might really happen; instead, she'd found the most outlandish possibilities she could come up with and focused on them. If you have a tendency to come down with the "what ifs," you can consciously train yourself to start thinking of the positives instead of the negatives.

What Are *You* Afraid Of?

To rid yourself of your fears you first need to decide what you're afraid of. Sit down with a pad and pencil and think about all the bad things you believe could happen if you began to make changes in your relationships, your physical environment, your prosperity, your spirituality, and your health. Write a header for each category you want to improve. Then, underneath each header write down what you want to change and what you're afraid might happen if you do. For example:

> I want to change jobs, but if I quit I might (not find another one; not like my new job any better; lose my accrued vacation time; not have such good health benefits).

> I want to move in with my girlfriend (or boyfriend), but if I do I might (find out that we're really not as compatible as I thought; realize that I'm just not ready to commit to the relationship; lose some of my freedom; have to take on more responsibility than I want; miss out on opportunities to meet someone else).

> I want to lose weight, but if I commit to doing that I might (find out it's harder than I thought; have trouble giving up foods I love; have to spend a lot of money joining a gym; lose weight and still not be any happier).

> I want to move to a different city, but if I do I might (lose touch with my friends; have trouble finding a job; not find as nice a house or apartment as I have now; discover it's a great place to visit but I don't like living there).

> I want to start my own home-based business, but if I decide to work from home I might (never go out; never be able to put my work aside and take time for myself; miss the interactions I have with my colleagues at work; spend too much time procrastinating and not enough time working).

> I really want a dog, but if I get one I might (hate walking it morning and night; discover it's more of a responsibility than I thought; find out I'm allergic to dogs).

You can use my list as a jumping-off point, but you need to think of the things that *you're* afraid of. Take as much time as you need to come up with every possible contingency. You don't have to do this all at once. Put it down and come back to it later if you want. When you're done, put your list in the kitchen sink (for safety) and light a match to it.

─── *A Word to the Wise* ───

As your fears burn away, repeat this affirmation:
I release these fears. I am no longer afraid to
make the changes I want to bring into my life.

Wash Away Negativity
and Get Rid of Your Fears

Sixty-five percent of the human body is made up of water. We can go as long as three weeks without food, but we have a hard time surviving more than three days without water. From ancient times, water has been a symbol of renewal, but it can also be dangerous and destructive. Water creates waves, and we humans live with waves of emotion—highs and lows. Sometimes we create rough seas for ourselves internally.

A SIMPLE RITUAL FOR
WASHING AWAY NEGATIVITY

Go to your sink and turn the tap on full. Hold your hands under the water (just be sure it isn't too hot) and envision any doubts you may have about the self-evaluation you're about to embark on going down the drain as you repeat to yourself, "I'm releasing all the negativity from my heart and my mind." And then mention each area where you might think you still doubt yourself or your ability to create positive change.

Once the doubt is washed away, you will be able to relinquish your fears. We all have fears, and many of those fears have to do with letting go of what we have because we can't be sure of what we might get instead. Very often, we're so afraid of making the wrong choice that we don't make any choice at all. But if we don't make any choice, we won't get anywhere. We'll just be standing at the crossroad forever trying to decide which direction to take.

I believe strongly in the power of water to wash away negativity. In fact, I keep a glass of water on the desk where I see clients, and, at the end of each day, I pour that water down the drain and turn on the tap as I visualize the clean, new water washing away the negative vibrations that may have been left behind by other people so that they don't cling to me.

Be Honest! Evaluate Yourself

The rituals I've described above are designed to help you focus on your determination to begin your self-evaluation. The place to begin being honest is always with yourself, so you must commit to that. I know it may not be easy. Many of us don't want to look too closely at ourselves in case we don't like what we see. But if you're not completely honest about who you are, you may be creating an unrealistic picture of what you want, and that is the best way to set yourself up for failure.

—————— *A Word to the Wise* ——————

We all spend a lot of time seeking knowledge,
but very often we're afraid of the truth.

I believe very strongly in writing things down. Once something is written in black and white it becomes harder to brush it aside or "forget" it. In addition, I believe that committing a desire or intention to paper increases its energy and makes it more likely that what you want or intend will actually come into your life. So before you go any further, get out a paper and pencil. At the top of the blank page write "Who and Where I Am Right Now." Beneath that headline make two columns. Label the left-hand column "Things I'm Happy With." Label the right-hand column "Things I Want to Change or Improve."

—————— *A Word to the Wise* ——————

It's okay to think big! If you're afraid to want
too much, you're likely to get less than you
need. But wanting a lot means working to
get it. We all create our own reality.

Now, start with the left-hand column and begin to make a list of all the things in your life that you are happy with. Just be sure when you do this that you make it about *you*. You might, for example, write:

1. I'm happy with my career choice.

2. I have many good friends.

3. I have a good sense of humor.

4. I love my blue eyes.

5. My mother and I have a very close relationship.

6. My children make me proud.

7. I love to read.

8. People tell me I'm very compassionate.

9. I'm a good listener.

10. I love to cook.

11. I'm a hard worker.

12. I'm proud that people perceive me as professional in my work.

13. I'm focused and pay attention to details.

14. My dog makes me smile.

Once you've thought of everything you can, move on to the right-hand column. You'll be able to add more items to the "happy" column as you think of them. Meanwhile, as you begin to determine what you want to change or improve, you'll already be in a positive frame of mind from thinking of so many good things, which means that you'll be more inclined to believe that change is possible.

─────── *A Word to the Wise* ───────

Be aware that you can only change yourself, not anyone else, and if you want to change your situation, you have to begin with yourself.

Among the things you want to change might be:

1. I want to get a better job.

2. I don't get out and socialize enough.

3. I'm unhappy with my weight.

4. I wish I were closer to my sister.

5. I need to become more financially secure.

6. I hate my hair.

7. I wish I were married.

8. I want to improve my tennis game.

9. I would love to start my own business.

10. I want to do something that makes a difference in the world.

11. I don't exercise enough.

12. I need to make more time to take care of myself.

13. I need to create more balance in my life.

14. I want to bring more spirituality into my life.

Remember that the suggestions I've made are simply to give you an idea of the kinds of things you *could* be putting on your own list. They are in no way intended to dictate what you should or should not be happy or unhappy about in your own life. Some of the items I suggest might seem trivial to you, others too broadly stated. But that's the way life is. Little things can make us very happy. Some of the changes we want to make may seem so all-encompassing that they appear impossible. But if we don't look at every aspect of our life we won't have all the information we need. We won't be able to make the best choices because we won't be aware of all the options that are available to us. Please remember, nothing is too big or too small to include on your lists.

Again, as with your list of fears, you don't have to do this in one marathon session. You can do it over several days or even weeks if you want, but you do have to find the quiet time to do it. I've found that too many people claim they don't have the time, but that's really just an excuse. If you have time to watch television or read a magazine, you have time to spend contemplating yourself. The problem is that many of us don't like to sit quietly and be alone with ourselves; it's a lot easier to be distracted.

A Word to the Wise

If you acknowledge the good things you have in your life, if you tell yourself how lucky you are to have those things, you'll be creating the mind-set you need to move toward the place you want to be.

Begin to Turn It Around

First, recognize the work you've done so far by adding "I am honest about my faults and my mistakes" to the positive column of your list. By acknowledging the things you want to change about yourself, you are actually turning a negative into a positive. When you are truly honest about yourself you are actually taking back your power. Think of it this way: if you blame other people or external circumstances for your situation, you are telling yourself that there's nothing you can do to change it. For many people that's taking the easy way out, because if you're not responsible for what happens to you, when things go wrong (as they will) it isn't your fault. But if you believe you're powerless to make changes, if that's what you store in your brain, that's what's going to happen. Once you take responsibility for where you are in your life, you are saying that you can make things different. When you believe that, it will happen.

A Word to the Wise

If you continue to sit at a broken traffic light waiting for it to change, you'll be sitting there forever.

One gentleman who came to see me was furious. I could feel his anger the moment he entered the room. He told me that he'd never attended college because his father was disabled and, as the oldest son, he had been forced to become the primary breadwinner at a very young age. By the time I met him he'd been working at a job he hated for more than twenty years, and he was still angry at his parents, who were both now deceased, for—as he saw it—depriving him of the opportunity to get more education and better himself.

After letting him vent, I pointed out to him that his father had surely not wanted to be sick and that his continuing to blame his parents for something that had happened so long ago wasn't really doing him any good. In fact, it was his pent-up anger rather than his family that was actually preventing him from moving forward in the present. He'd been focusing so much on his anger that he had no energy left to focus on his goal.

His dream had always been to become a chef and open his own restaurant, so I asked him why he didn't take cooking classes in the evening after work. He thought about it for a moment and confessed that it had never occurred to him to do that. But he thought it was something he could realistically consider.

Once my client was able to accept responsibility for the choices he'd made, he wrote a letter of apology to his mother and father, which helped him to let go of his anger. Then he looked into local culinary schools and started to take the cooking classes he'd delayed for so long. Eventually he was able to open his own restaurant and has now also started a small winery in Northern California.

It's a truism worth repeating that no one is perfect and no one is born into a perfect situation. Too often too many of us seem to forget that. We think that other people don't have to work as hard as we do for what they have or that we're the only one who is unhappy about some aspect of our life. Not so! What is true, however, is that some of us are better than others at admitting our mistakes and forgiving ourselves for making them. Most of us are pretty good at beating ourselves up. The first key to change actually involves taking three steps:

1. **Acknowledge your faults or mistakes.** Accept the fact that we all have faults and we all make mistakes. They only get in our way if we let them.

2. **Forgive yourself.** Being angry with yourself for something you did in the past is a waste of energy.

3. **Affirm your commitment to change.** The only reason to stay angry with yourself is if you don't do anything to change.

─── *A Word to the Wise* ───

Life is one long learning experience.
The more honest we are with and about
ourselves, the more we will learn.

WRITE YOUR OWN LETTER OF APOLOGY

It's hard for some of us to apologize. We just don't know where to begin. Here's a sample letter of apology that you can use to help you get started writing one of your own.

> Dear (Mom, Dad, or whomever you want to forgive),
>
> I'm sorry that I've been blaming you all these years for (you fill in the blank).
>
> I've really been thinking about it and I now realize that you always did what you believed was best for me and that I've been blaming you as a way to avoid taking responsibility for the choices I made for myself.
>
> I'm making a promise to myself not to do that anymore, and this letter is to let you know that I'm not angry anymore. I hope you will also forgive me for the misplaced anger I've been harboring for so long.
>
> With love,
>
> _____

Once you've written your letter, settle in a comfortable chair in a quiet place. Take a couple of deep breaths and read your letter aloud. If you're sincere about what you've written, you'll actually feel as if a weight is being lifted from your heart.

Now put your letter away safely so that, if you ever feel that anger creeping back in, you can take it out and reread it as a way to reaffirm your intention to change.

Of course, you can (and should) write as many letters to as many people as you feel you want or need to.

Anger Is a Waste of Energy

I remember the forty-one-year-old woman who came to me because she knew her biological clock was ticking; she wanted a family, but she hadn't yet been able to find a life partner. She owned a very successful business manufacturing scented candles that were sold throughout the world, but she hadn't been able to find the same kind of success in her personal life. When I talked with her, she told me a bit about her personal history. Among the things I learned was the fact that her father had wanted her to be a lawyer and had never understood or supported her entrepreneurial spirit. As a result—even though he had died years before—she was still harboring a lot of anger toward him and was determined to show him how successful she was. All of her drive and energy were, therefore, being channeled into her business, and she had nothing left over to invest in romance or personal relationships. First, I explained, she needed to become aware of the fact that she was angry with her father. Then she needed to come to grips with the fact that her anger was actually preventing her from getting everything she wanted out of life. And finally, she needed to let go of her anger and turn all that wasted energy into something positive for herself.

It's easy to walk around angry all the time. We can all find something to be angry about. *No one understands me! How come Joe got promoted and I didn't? Here I am on vacation and it hasn't stopped raining! Why am I always the one who gets stuck doing the dishes? My stupid husband forgot our anniversary—again!*

The problem is that being angry isn't going to get you anywhere. In fact, it's probably going to make things worse because people aren't going to *want* to understand you. No one is going to promote an angry person. You'll make sure to ruin whatever fun you might have had on your vacation. Your family will stay out of the kitchen and you'll never get help with the dishes. Your relationship with your husband is going to become even more strained. In other words, being angry never cured anything.

Anger, jealousy, and insecurity often go hand in hand. Instead of staying angry, it would be more productive to examine your own issues and try to find out why you might be jealous or insecure. One client of mine was always angry because, in her mind, everyone else seemed to be getting something that she deserved. When we began to look for the source of her jealousy, we were able to determine that because she came from a large family and was the eldest of six brothers and sisters she never felt that she was getting the attention she deserved and believed that she was always, in effect, the neglected child.

Things don't change, only the way you look at them.
—**Carlos Castaneda**

Sometimes we actually have a right to be angry, like Donna, a client who found out at her husband's funeral that he had a second family she knew nothing about. Donna and her husband had a son and a daughter, but at the funeral another woman came forward and introduced her to two other children fathered by Donna's husband. Donna's immediate reaction was to be furious with her husband and

HAVE AN EMOTIONAL TANTRUM

If you're walking around with a lot of pent-up anger, give yourself permission to let it all out. Go into the bathroom, turn the water on, and yell if you want. Have your little rage and get it out of your system. You'll be amazed how good it feels afterward.

Now, tell yourself that's it. No more. It's gone. Let the anger flow away with the tap water and decide that you're going to move on. You can do it.

equally furious with the woman, whom she immediately decided was a gold digger. Finally, it was Donna's own daughter who made her realize that, whatever the two adults might have done, the ones who would suffer from her anger would be not only Donna herself but also two innocent children.

What we all need to do is find a way to get rid of our anger. The longer we hold on to it, the less likely we'll be to find peace. Not so long ago a man called in to my radio program whose wife had left him for another woman. All he kept asking was when *they* were going to break up. The only road to happiness he saw for himself lay in his ex-wife's potential *un*happiness. In effect, he was choosing to cling to his anger.

If you can't seem to let go of anger, try to figure out what you can do to change that. If you're angry about something that's beyond your control, like the weather, or something you know in your heart is really stupid, like not finding your favorite ice cream in the supermarket, you've just got to learn to let it go. If you can't reason yourself out of it, do something to get your mind in a different place. Go for a run, work out at the gym, or do something that calms you down. For some people it could be gardening or listening to music, for others it might be cleaning out dresser drawers. Buy yourself some flowers. Sit on the beach and listen to the sound of the waves. Take a nice, long, spiritual bath with calming lavender oil. Personally, sailing always relaxes me. If I'm not doing the actual sailing, I like to sit at the front of the boat and let my mind flow with the water. I can actually feel the stress and tension flowing out of my body. Whatever it takes, just do it. My own affirmation for releasing anger is to say, "My mind is a happy place. I'm peaceful. I refuse to get upset about things I can't control."

If it's something serious, you need to tell yourself that your anger is never going to improve the situation; instead, it's just adding to your stress. If whatever happened is in the past, it's already happened and there's nothing you can do to change it, so you might as well let it go. If you continue to bring up the past all you'll get out of it is bad memories. If it's happening in the present, you have the power to do something differently instead of staying stuck and staying mad. Refusing to be controlled by your anger is what will give you the freedom to take control of your future.

The Key to Your Present Lies in Your Past

Many of us are so caught up in the past that we can't focus on the present. Instead, we keep repeating familiar patterns. Whether or not we're aware of it, significant people and events in our life profoundly affect the way we think. If, for example, a member of your family or someone close to you told you every day of your life growing up that you were dumb and you'd never make anything of yourself, guess what? Chances are that you eventually began to think of yourself as not very bright, which caused you to lose confidence in your own ability to make good decisions. And if that's what you were thinking, it's undoubtedly what came true.

The person who told you that probably didn't do it on purpose, but even if he or she did, there's not much you can do to change anyone else. You can, however, forgive that person for his or her mistake and affirm to yourself that you will no longer allow anyone else to determine how you view yourself. As a way to affirm your intention, write a letter like the one on page 30 to both forgive the person from your past and take responsibility for your choices now and in the future.

Or, conversely, if someone continuously told you how pretty you were, you probably grew up with a positive self-image—at least where looks were concerned. You can now thank him or her for that and take ownership of the belief.

Have you hung on to a dead-end job for years because your parents taught you that it was more important to be secure than to be happy in your work? Have you let people push you around because that's how your dad treated your mom?

Look at the lists you made of the positive and negative aspects of your life and ask yourself who or what in your past may have been responsible for teaching you to have those thoughts and feelings. It's important to understand that until you are able to recognize and acknowledge how you got to be where you are you won't be able to move forward.

Generally speaking, we all have some story that we tell ourselves about our life. It may be a story you made up or some fairy tale that was handed down to you by your parents. Since the story was made up in the first place, you can change the ending any way you want. You just have to start telling yourself a new story and keep repeating it until you believe it. Changing the story is the first step toward changing yourself.

WHAT'S YOUR STORY?

Here are two versions of a personal story. See how the first version got written and how the revision changes the outcome.

Version 1

My friends all tell me I'm a fun person to be with because I can always make them laugh by laughing at myself. Ever since I was a little kid my mom always told me that I needed to have a "good personality" because I certainly wasn't pretty enough to get by on looks alone. I'm happy that I have a lot of friends but sometimes I just wish that I didn't always have to try so hard to be the life of the party. I'm just afraid that if I let them know when I am sad or scared they won't like me anymore.

Version 2

I used to think that I always had to be the life of the party because when I was a kid my mom was always telling me that I wasn't as pretty as the other little girls. But now I realize that even though I may not be a raving beauty, many people do find me attractive, and I'm also caring and intelligent. When I finally got up the courage to stop laughing at myself before anyone else could laugh at me, I realized that people really do like me for who I am and they didn't want me always to be putting myself down like that. I know that my mom was just trying to keep me from getting hurt. I wish that she'd been able to find some other way to do that, but I believe she did what she thought was best. I forgive her for not knowing any better and I forgive myself for not loving myself more.

Have you been telling yourself a sad story? If so, get out a pencil and write yourself a story with a happy ending.

My Story, Version 1

_____

_____

_____

_____

_____

_____

_____

_____

My Story, Version 2

_____

_____

_____

_____

_____

_____

_____

_____

No Mistake Is Irreversible

Sometimes we're so conditioned by the poor choices we've made in the past that we come to believe any choice we make will be the wrong choice. Thinking that way then becomes a vicious cycle, because we are thinking so negatively that anything we bring into our life is sure to be negative. We become like Joe Btfsplk, the character in *Li'l Abner* who walked around with his own personal rain cloud over his head. As the cycle continues we become more and more certain that we can't make good choices and so we become paralyzed with fear.

If that's the frame of mind you're in, you need to begin thinking more like Thomas Edison, who said, "If I find ten thousand ways something won't work, I haven't failed. I am not discouraged, because every wrong attempt discarded is another step forward." Edison understood something very important: Sometimes when we think we've made a mistake, it isn't really a mistake at all. It's just something we needed to experience in order to get to the next level. On page 21 I gave you a simple ritual for washing away negative thoughts. Any time you feel fear creeping back in, return to that ritual and wash your fears down the drain.

I believe that our past extends back through previous lives and that we never stop learning. The key is to learn one lesson at a time so that we can move on to the next. If we don't take a good look at ourselves and the choices we've made in the past, our mistakes will keep repeating themselves like a bad case of mental and emotional heartburn.

Determine not to make the same mistakes again, then forgive

yourself and move on. To help you with that, repeat the following affirmation: "I am allowing myself to forgive myself for mistakes I have made. I am releasing the guilt. I no longer blame myself for what happened in the past."

—— *A Word to the Wise* ——

We all deserve to be happy. Whether or not we achieve that depends on how hard we're willing to work at being happy. By not dealing with our past we are allowing unresolved emotional issues to get in our way.

Write a Personal Mission Statement for Your Life

Once you've figured out where you are and how you got there, write a personal mission statement to clarify where you want to go from here. Be as clear and specific as you can, not only about what you want to achieve but how you plan to achieve it. Once your life's mission is down on paper you'll have it to refer to if you think you're wandering off course. You don't want to lose sight of your goals and you don't want to lose yourself. The point is to remain true to the best self you can possibly be.

To help you complete your personal mission, in the chapters that follow we'll be looking at five key aspects of your life—your relationships, your physical environment, your prosperity, your spiritual strength, and your emotional and physical well-being.

You're on a mission to fill your personal treasure chest, so you need to stay focused and follow the path even though you may stumble or need to hack your way through some underbrush along the way. In the end, I assure you, the rewards will be worth the journey.

My Personal Mission Statement

_____

_____

_____

_____

_____

_____

_____

_____

_____

_____

_____

A Checklist for Choices to Put in Your Treasure Chest

✓ *Say an affirmation as you burn away negative thoughts.*

✓ *Say an affirmation as you wash away your fears.*

✓ *Make a list of your strengths and/or things that make you happy.*

✓ *Make a list of your problems and/or things you want to change.*

✓ *Take a good look at your past to determine how it is influencing your present.*

✓ *Say an affirmation to forgive yourself for past mistakes.*

✓ *Make a pledge to move on.*

✓ *Write a mission statement for your life.*

GATHER YOUR SOUL MATES

When relationships are positive, they energize you and buoy you up; when they're negative, they can deplete you and pull you down. People who enhance and energize our lives—our soul mates—are treasures to be cherished and nurtured. Those who limit and drain our positivity, however, may be preventing us from creating the abundance that could be ours.

If you're serving a literal prison term, you don't get to choose who is assigned to be your cell mate, but sometimes the people you *voluntarily* bring into your life can make it seem as if you're serving a life sentence. If that's your situation, it's probably time to start planning a prison break.

Every person, all the events of your life are there because you have drawn them there. What you choose to do with them is up to you.

—Richard Bach, *Illusions*

What Is a Soul Mate?

In his *Symposium*, Plato describes a soul mate as the missing half that will complete us. The renowned psychic Edgar Cayce described a soul mate as someone of the opposite sex with whom we were joined in a previous incarnation and with whom we are seeking to reunite. I believe that a soul mate is someone with whom we have shared past lives and with whom we have a deep karmic connection. I also sometimes say that a soul mate is the person who has the key that fits your lock. If you're constantly struggling to make a relationship work, you can be fairly certain that you haven't yet found the right key, and no matter how much you turn it one way or the other and try to jiggle it up and down to open the lock, it isn't going happen.

When you meet a soul mate the key will fit. You will feel almost as if you were looking in a mirror; you'll recognize what's being reflected back at you. There will be an immediate deep and natural connection, as I felt when I met my wife. From the first moment, I felt that I knew her; I knew who she was emotionally and how she thought. I knew there was a past spiritual and emotional connection between us, and I could see right away what our future together would be.

You and your soul mate probably won't always agree on everything (which would be boring in any case), but you'll want the same things in life. You'll bring out the best in each other, nurture each other, and each of you will get pleasure from watching the other grow.

I believe that one of the truest ways to know that you've met a soul mate is that you'll always want the best for the other person and you'll know that you want to grow old with him or her. Of course, the road you travel together won't always be smooth; there may be detours or rough spots along the way. But if the person with whom you're making the journey is truly a soul mate, you'll want to do whatever it takes to get yourselves back on track, whether that means getting professional help or simply communicating your needs and feelings more clearly—and listening more closely to the needs and feelings of your partner.

—— *A Word to the Wise* ——

To avoid mistaking a cell mate for a soul mate, get in touch with who you are and what you value. In order to recognize a soul mate you first need to know yourself.

Soul Mates and Cell Mates Are All Around Us

Soul mates or cell mates can crop up anywhere in your life—not just in a sexual or romantic relationship. I know that's what people generally think of when they say they've found their soul mate, but the fact is that you can have many different soul mates in various aspects of your life, and no one can ever have too many.

In the business world, we often talk about mentors, people who have taken us under their wing and helped us to succeed in our chosen career. Or sometimes we have a colleague with whom we work easily and productively, someone who has great ideas and brings out our own creativity. These people, too, are soul mates. And so are the friends who we know will stick with us through our darkest days, whom we can count on to be there when we need them, who can make us laugh and lift us up when we're down, the ones we never tire of being with.

Take for example Natalie and Karen, two young women I met when I stopped into the new food shop they had opened near my home. As we were chatting, they told me that their parents had been friends and they'd known each other virtually from birth and had grown up almost like sisters. Of course, it doesn't always work out that just because parents are friendly their children will also get along, but Natalie and Karen were obviously soul mates. Their friendship had grown closer as they matured. Now, as young women, they understood and trusted each other completely and held similar beliefs about what was important in life. As I was leaving, I wished them luck and told them I was sure that their new business would thrive.

Maybe as a child you had a favorite aunt or uncle, someone you always loved visiting because he or she made you feel special. Or perhaps you've always felt closer to one sibling than another. I'm sure you love all your siblings but sometimes you feel a kind of bond with one who seems so much more like you. Sometimes a mother or father will look at a child and say, "He (or she) is exactly like me. I see myself in him." That child, too, is a soul mate. It's not that parents don't love all their children, but not all children are our soul mates.

A life mate should be your soul mate,
but not all soul mates are life mates.

Soul Mates and Cell Mates You Choose

Soul mates are those who help your soul grow. I hope that most of the people you invite into your life enhance and empower you with their positive energy, expand your heart and your mind, and encourage you to become the best you can be. But if you're involved in relationships whose negativity is weighing you down, you probably need to think about why you got involved with these people in the first place and whether you still want them in your life. That may sound harsh, but, if so, it's a harsh truth.

We don't always take the time to really think about the people with whom we surround ourselves. Too often we let relationships drag on just because they've become familiar and we seem to have invested a lot of time and energy into them—even though they may be difficult or actually detrimental to our mental, physical, and spiritual well-being.

Sharon, a client of mine, was a bright, attractive woman in her mid-fifties who had been in a relationship with a married man for twenty-five years. For all those years, he continually told her he was going to leave his wife, and she—against all odds—continued to believe him. The fact that she *wanted* to believe was clouding her better judgment.

Consequently, she kept thinking that if she cut off the relationship and moved on, that would be just the time when he'd actually do what he kept promising and she would have missed out on her moment.

When her lover died suddenly of a heart attack, Sharon couldn't even attend his funeral. At that point she realized that she'd been living all those years waiting for the crumbs he tossed her way and that she'd given up any chance of having a family of her own. When she finally came to see me, she was both bereft by the loss of her lover and bewildered by where she now found herself—effectively with no life of her own. As we talked, it became clear that she had grown up with an absentee father and that she had been re-creating that relationship with her lover—endlessly waiting and hoping for a relationship that was not to be.

When I explained to Sharon that her father was not and never could be her lover, and that she had imposed her unfulfilled childhood hopes upon yet another man who was destined to disappoint her, she broke down in tears. But, ultimately, that was a life-changing moment of clarity for her—one that allowed her to finally let go of a past she couldn't change so that she *could* change her future. I didn't hear from Sharon for several months after that, until she phoned one day to tell me that she'd met a wonderful man who was devoted to her and her alone and that they were planning to spend the rest of their lives together.

Another young woman, named Andrea, was also deeply involved with a cell mate, to the point where she had become obsessed, thinking about him virtually every moment of every day. Unfortunately, however, her obsessive devotion was not returned, and one day the man who was the object of her affections simply disappeared from her life without any explanation or even a good-bye. Andrea was left with a deep emotional wound that she simply couldn't heal, which is why she came to me. It took some time, but I was finally able to help her realize that this man, however much she thought she loved him, was not and never would be her soul mate. She hadn't been seeing him clearly; her own feelings had blinded her to the fact that he simply didn't return those feelings. In other words, the relationship that she saw had been largely a creation of her own imagination. Once she was able to remove those blinders, she could begin to let go of the fantasy and begin to face the reality of the situation. Instead of seeing only what she had lost, she could look at what she had gained in terms of self-knowledge. Facing reality meant that she would be able to make another, better choice for herself when it came time to begin a new relationship.

Soul mates, as I've said, want and help us to grow, but even cell mates can help us to grow if we are willing to look inward and recognize what they are teaching us about ourselves. It takes courage to remove the blinders and take a good look not only at ourselves but also at the people we're bringing into our life. Doing that, however, can ultimately help us to turn our life around so that it becomes much richer and more rewarding.

What Kinds of People
Are You Bringing into *Your* Life?

If you are now wondering about the true value of any of your own relationships, it's time to stop and take stock. What kind of people are you bringing into your life?

Are they

Sensitive?

Caring?

Loving?

Supportive?

Do they lift you up when you're feeling down?

Do they make you feel important?

Do they show respect for your boundaries?

Do they accept you for exactly who you are?

These are the people to be treasured.

Or, are they

Selfish?

Overbearing?

Bossy?

Negative?

Controlling?

Addictive?

Codependent?

Abusive?

Do they put you down?

Do they always think they're right?

Do they refuse to commit?

In which case you're collecting fool's gold.

✦　✦　✦

Make a list of all the important people in every area of your life, the people you are choosing to spend time with. Now, make an actual checklist and put the pluses in one column, the minuses in another.

NAME OF PERSON

Positive Qualities in Relationship	Negative Qualities in Relationship
+	−
+	−
+	−
+	−

To help you assess your relationships accurately, consider these questions:

> ➤ How do you feel when you're with each one of these people?

> ➤ When you think about being with him or her are you excited and energized or does it feel like a chore?

> ➤ What are you gaining from the relationship?

> ➤ What are you giving?

> ➤ Is it costing more than it's worth in terms of your emotional energy?

> ➤ Have you learned something from being with this person?

> ➤ Are you still learning?

Seeing that balance sheet right in front of you in black and white may be all you need to decide whether the relationship is one to treasure or one to toss. In the pages that follow, I'll be explaining how to extricate yourself from painful and/or negative relationships, no matter how tightly bound you may now feel to the other person.

Letting go can sometimes be a painful process, but it is one that ultimately frees you. When problems occur it's usually because you're trying to loosen the ties without breaking them completely. You may, for example, make excuses by hanging on to the good memories, such as a happy anniversary celebration or a gift you were given, as a way to mitigate the problems that preceded or followed it. The only way to really achieve clarity is by remembering *all* of the relationship and determining not to repeat your mistakes.

A Word to the Wise

We all get "vibes" when we meet new people.
The trouble is that we often don't listen to them.
Start paying more attention to those feelings
and you'll be more likely to avoid becoming
involved in potentially toxic relationships.

Do You See a Pattern Emerging?

A pattern is anything that keeps repeating itself, like rows of climbing roses on wallpaper. Sometimes, if you're standing too close or only see a small piece of the wallpaper, you don't really see the pattern. What you need to do is step back so that you can get a better perspective on the big picture. And the same is true of your relationships.

If you keep gravitating to the same kinds of people—for example, friends who boss you around or bosses who make you feel inadequate—if the people with whom you form intimate relationships tend to be unavailable, unresponsive, or unloving, you may be repeating a pattern. Did you grow up with a bossy sister or a big brother who was always putting you down? Was your dad undemonstrative or often absent—emotionally if not physically? If those are the kinds of relationships you know best (even though they're not the best for you), you may be repeating them without being aware of it.

The problem is that too many of us don't want to see our negative patterns for what they really are. The lessons may be right in front of us, staring us in the face, but we turn our back and refuse to recognize them. Maybe—like my client who couldn't let go of her married lover—your father abandoned you when you were a child, so you are constantly drawn to men who are unavailable or who refuse to commit. Maybe your father was charming when he was drunk and, subconsciously, you now equate drinking with charm and therefore draw in a succession of charming alcoholics. The problem is that your father may also have been irresponsible, incapable of holding down a job, and a poor provider. Are the charming alcoholics in your life today following that same pattern? If so, you need to start attracting a different kind of man.

Or maybe you're a young man who keeps getting involved with clinging, overly dependent women. When you stop to think about it, do any of these women remind you of your mother? Did you love your mother very much? Did you try to act the part of the "little man" for her, perhaps to make up for your absent or less-than-dependable father?

Brad, another of my clients, was a charming and talented gay man who'd been raised by an extremely overbearing mother. Among his many talents, Brad was an extremely gifted pianist and had always dreamed of playing piano as a way to earn a living. His mother, however, had decided that this wasn't a good career choice. In order to discourage him, she continually denigrated his musical talent and, in general, did whatever it took to be sure he didn't succeed.

The first man Brad became involved with turned out to be a clone of his mother. He, too, was controlling and overbearing, and he decided that Brad ought to become an interior designer. In fact, Brad was very good at the career his lover had assigned him, but he hated it. It took many years of therapy for him to see the pattern he'd been repeating and to get to the point where he could assert himself and follow his childhood dream. Brad is now a very successful professional pianist.

If you seem to keep making bad choices and bringing new cell mates into your life, you probably need to ask yourself if your current cell mate is taking the place of someone in your past. On an unconscious level, you may be thinking that you can change your past relationship and make it better this time around. Or you may simply be viewing your past relationship in an unrealistic light, which means that you won't be seeing your present relationships for what they really are.

What We Put Out Is What We Bring In

I don't believe in accidents, and I believe that the universe puts people in our path for a reason, because we have something to learn from them that could change the kind of energy we're putting out—because, of course, what we put out determines what we bring in.

I'll never forget the young woman I'll call Sarah who came to me three months before she was to be married. Sarah was a lovely blonde with bright blue eyes that didn't seem to reflect the joy and excitement I'd expect to see in a young woman about to be married. Seeing that look of trepidation in her eyes, I asked, "Do you know why you're getting married?" I know my unexpected question caught her off guard, but she admitted that she couldn't really answer me. I told her she was making a big mistake and would undoubtedly wake up a month after the wedding and realize she shouldn't have done it. Sarah was shocked; she couldn't believe that I'd say something like that, but I believe that on a deep gut level she knew I was right—or else why would she have come to me for confirmation of her decision in the first place?

Sure enough, she came back several months later and said, "You know, I should have listened to you. I'd have saved myself a lot of trouble and a lot of money." What Sarah hadn't realized was that, because she'd had a difficult upbringing, she was yearning for a family, and she'd married this man not for himself but to become part of his family. She's now happily remarried, but she needed to go through that first relationship before she was able to see her truth and get it right the next time.

One problem with being unconsciously driven by our own negative patterns is that when we do come face-to-face with a soul mate, we may not recognize him or her and therefore may walk right on by.

Sandra, for example, was married to a man of whom her father had never approved. Her father was constantly criticizing her husband and pointing out the many ways in which he was lacking. Although he was a perfectly nice man and a good husband, over time Sandra actually began to see her husband through her father's eyes and wound up divorcing him. The truth was that her controlling father had simply resented the fact that there was another man in her life and never would have approved of *anyone* his daughter married. Finally, once her father died and was no longer there to constantly reinforce his negative judgments, Sandra was able to see she'd made a terrible mistake. She had the courage to admit it to her ex-husband, and—happily for her— he had never stopped loving her and they were able to reconcile. The moral of this story is that we make it hard for ourselves and that our relatives, whoever they are, can only control our lives if we allow them to.

We all tend to be drawn to what is familiar, but if what is familiar is negative, we need to change that. If you can become conscious of repeating negative patterns from your past, you will start to see your alcoholic father, dependent mother, your bossy sister, or criticizing brother more realistically, and once you do that you will be able to change the script that's been subconsciously running in your head. You'll be rewriting the story you've been telling yourself and shifting the psychic energy that creates your reality.

Forgive and Let Go

Esther came to me because her father had died and she was unable to come to terms with the fact that they hadn't spoken to each other for almost thirty years. Esther had never tried to resolve their original problem; instead she had simply written him off. Because of their rift, her children had never been able to know their grandfather. When I made contact with her father in the spirit world, he said that he now realized what a great and tragic mistake he had made by losing out on having a relationship not only with his daughter but with his grand-children. Esther and her father had both been stubborn, and their stubbornness had prevented them from forgiving each other so that they could both move on. Even worse, however, their animosity had also estranged Esther from her mother, who found it difficult, under the circumstances, to remain close to her daughter. Her father now wanted to tell Esther that he hoped she would be able to forgive and repair that relationship before it was too late.

——— *A Word to the Wise* ———

Never be afraid to say you're wrong.
Never be afraid to say you're sorry.

Neil, another client of mine, seemed like a nice enough guy, but every time he got to the point in a relationship where he would have to make a commitment, he would do something to sabotage it. He'd done this over and over, and in the process he knew he had hurt several people. Still, he didn't seem able to change the self-defeating pattern he'd established. As we talked, I found out that his own mother had abandoned him as a child. It became clear that, subconsciously, Neil was now determined to be the one who did the abandoning rather than be the one left behind. In the end, he was hurting people because he, himself, had been hurt. But harboring that kind of unconscious anger just traps you in a vicious cycle and holds you back from finding or recognizing any soul mate who might come your way.

If you can acknowledge the root causes of what's holding you back, you'll be able to forgive yourself for whatever mistakes you have made. Once you forgive yourself it also becomes easier to forgive those who may have hurt you.

AFFIRM YOUR COMMITMENT TO CHANGE

To help reinforce your commitment to change, practice the following forgiveness ritual.

First, take a good look at your most recent relationships. Let's say that you continue to get involved with domineering, overbearing people. Write down your experience: "My last girlfriend was so controlling that I always had to account for every minute of my time. She called me at least eight times a day."

Now, really think about what pattern you might be repeating. "My mother did the same thing to me because my parents' marriage was so bad that she lived through me, for me, and wanted to *be* me. Because of that I began to believe that this was the kind of relationship I deserved in my life." Note that when you do this, you're not blaming your girlfriend for the difficult relationship, nor are you blaming your mother. You're actually acknowledging that the choices were yours.

Now, find a quiet spot, make yourself comfortable, relax, and take control of your breathing as you repeat, either out loud or to yourself, the following affirmation and commitment to change: "I forgive myself for making bad choices about my relationships in the past. I forgive my mother for the choices she made. From now on I will make new choices. I will not allow what happened in the past to determine my present or my future."

You can also write down your affirmation to change and store it away for future reference and safekeeping.

DESCRIBE YOUR PERFECT SOUL MATE

Once you've affirmed your commitment to change negative patterns, sit down in a quiet place and imagine your perfect soul mate. Make a list of as many characteristics as you can think of for the person you would like to bring into your life. (To get started, look back to the list of positive characteristics on page 50.) Be extremely clear in your description. Don't leave out any details, no matter how minor they may seem. Height, eye color, hair color, interests, personality, background, ethnicity, profession—everything matters and there are no right or wrong answers. Just be very sure and accept the fact that this is what you want. Write it all down in the space below or, if you prefer, in a notebook.

My Soul Mate Is . . .

_____

_____

_____

_____

_____

_____

_____

_____

_____

_____

_____

_____

_____

_____

_____

_____

_____

_____

You can also cut out pictures of people who resemble the soul mate of your dreams. Add photos of people whose mental, spiritual, and emotional qualities you seek in a soul mate.

Remember that you can have different soul mates for different aspects of your life, so the boss of your dreams or your bosom friend may have different qualities from those of your ideal lover or mate.

Store away your descriptions and your photos and refer to them often. When you meet someone you think might be a soul mate, look at your treasures to see how he or she measures up.

—— *A Word to the Wise* ——

It's easier to settle for less than you want
or need because then whatever you get is a
bonus. It's easier to fail than it is to succeed.
Don't be afraid to step beyond the familiar.

Don't Be Afraid to Ask

Keep telling yourself that you deserve to have soul mates in your life. You don't have to be afraid to want something. We all deserve to find fulfillment in every area of life, and we can—so long as we create the positive energy to pull it in.

Too often, however, if we've been in a series of unfulfilling or destructive relationships we begin to expect that this is what it's always going to be like. If you think that way, you're probably right, because your thoughts have energy and your thought processes affect what's going on in your life. Once you've done the inner work with the help of this book, however, you'll certainly find yourself in a much better place.

Put Yourself Out There

Asking for the person you want to bring into your life and affirming your intention is an important first step, but remember that God (or Karma or the universe) helps those who help themselves. Your soul mate is probably not the UPS delivery person ringing your doorbell, so you need to get up off the sofa and out of the house to meet him or her.

There's a lot of talk these days about networking, but the concept is really quite simple: put yourself in a place where you're likely to meet someone whose qualities you admire and whose interests are compatible with yours. Go back and review the list of qualities you seek in a soul mate. If you're looking for someone who loves to eat, join a cooking class. If you hate people who drink, don't go to a bar. If you think football is boring, stay away from sporting events. If you love to read, join a book club. Do you love animals? Why not volunteer at your local shelter? One woman I know found her soul mate through their mutual love of horseback riding, another through a love of running marathons.

Since a soul mate is someone who thinks and feels the way you do, you ought to feel comfortable in the situations where you're most likely to meet him or her. If you're not, there's a good chance that you haven't yet been honest about who you are and what you want. Take another look at the self-assessment you've completed. Is there something about yourself you've been avoiding? Have you been putting roadblocks in your own path? Think about those patterns you've discovered. Are you

AFFIRM YOUR HEART'S DESIRE

To help ensure you get what your heart (and soul) desires, affirm your intentions to yourself and to your higher power. Whether it's the love of your life, the boss of your dreams, or the friend with whom you can share your greatest hopes and deepest fears, write down what you want to bring in *as if* it were yours right now.

I deserve love and I want to accept it now.

I get excited every day about finding that kind of connection.

I release any fear I have that it's not going to happen.

Commit your intention to paper, keep it safe, and repeat those words each night before you go to bed so that they take root in your subconscious as you sleep. It is my belief that the subconscious is the gateway to the universe.

about to embark on another dead end? If so, stop right now! Pull over to the side of the road, take a good, hard look at where your emotions have been leading you, and try to find another route.

Not so long ago I received a letter from a woman named Martha, who had come to me as a client more than ten years ago. I remembered her as a pretty but troubled woman who had exuded sadness. In her letter Martha reminded me that, all those years before, I had told her she would meet a man in uniform who was divorced, with two children, and he would be her soul mate. At the time, she was involved in a bad relationship, but I assured her that she would finally get it right and that she'd be happily married, which had always been her dream.

In her letter, Martha went on to say that our meeting had finally gotten her to realize that she'd been in one unhappy relationship after another and once she'd reevaluated herself, she was able to see that she had always been settling for less than she wanted and deserved. While she engaged in that process of reevaluation, she was invited to attend her nephew's graduation from the Merchant Marine Academy. She didn't really want to go, she wasn't feeling very social, but based on our conversation and her reassessment of herself, she decided to put herself out there. And what do you think happened? One of her nephew's instructors turned out to be just the person I'd told her she would meet. Based on my description and her newfound self-awareness, Martha recognized her soul mate, whereas previously she might have passed him right by.

Another client, whom I'll call Louise, was in a terrible marriage. When she came to me she was angry and confused. She'd just found out that her husband, Ed, had been having an affair. She told me that her twenty-fifth high school reunion was coming up in a couple of months and she'd been thinking of a classmate named Tom whom she'd always liked and who had always been kind to her even thought they'd never actually dated. She figured that the upcoming reunion had triggered her thoughts of Tom, but she still wasn't sure whether or not she should try to save her marriage, and she wanted to know whether I thought she should go to the reunion. Of course, I told her that her intuition was trying to guide her and that she should go.

When she got there, she ran into Tom, who told her that he'd been thinking about her, too. It turned out that he had recently been divorced, but at the time neither one of them was willing to let the relationship develop into anything more than a happy reunion. It wasn't until after Louise finally divorced Ed that she got back in touch with Tom, who then told her that he'd always been attracted to her in high school but had been afraid to approach her because she was so popular and he didn't want to risk being rejected.

Tom and Louise were soul mates, but it took them twenty-five years to listen to their hearts and make the connection that had been fated for them. Sometimes it can take that long, but it's never too late—and when you do finally find your soul mate, it will have been worth the wait.

All Relationships Take Work

We all dream of leading a charmed life with our soul mate, but for most of us it doesn't turn out quite that way.

As human beings we are all fallible, which means that no relationship is going to be perfect all the time, even if it is with a soul mate. All relationships take work and compromise if they are to survive. Take for example the case of my client who was one of the most successful and high-powered women on Wall Street. Even when she met her perfect mate, she was so driven, so rigid, and so set in her ways that she couldn't do what was necessary to nurture and cultivate the relationship. She was used to having other people do what she wanted, and she expected her partner to adjust to her but didn't do anything to make room for him in her life. As a result, the relationship didn't last, and she went through five more years alone before seeking the therapy that finally allowed her to acknowledge her own problems. By then, however, she had lost the one person who she believed had been perfect for her. The lesson my client's story has to teach is that it's always better to work on yourself now, before you've lost something valuable in your life.

In another situation, exactly the opposite happened. Mark, a successful international businessman who spent much of his time jetting back and forth to meetings around the globe, met the woman who was his soul mate and was able to reorganize his priorities. At first Mark thought that sending the corporate jet to fetch her would be all that it took to keep her in his life—wherever life might take him. But she made it clear that she wanted to spend more time with him, not his pilot or waiting for him to get out of a business meeting, and when Mark realized he might lose her, he was able to make the necessary adjustments, learn to enjoy a vacation now and then, and figure out how to make another person feel welcome and appreciated in his hectic life.

And finally, there were the twin sisters who had grown up in a dysfunctional family and, because of that, had become so close to each other that now, as adults, they were both neglecting their husbands and putting their marriages in jeopardy. They lived in neighboring towns and spent almost all their time together. Even when they were with their husbands, the men felt as if they were expendable. Because the two women had always been each other's primary support, they had come to believe, without ever realizing it, that they didn't really need anyone else as long as they had each other. I had to explain to them that our hearts and souls are infinitely expansive and that becoming closer and more caring with their spouses didn't mean that they couldn't also be just as close to each other. With that realization, they were able to bring their husbands into their inner circle of love and show them the same care they had been showing each other.

Whether it's with a lover, a friend, or a relative, a relationship is a living, organic entity that needs care and nurturing if it is to thrive. If you want someone in your life, you need to open yourself up and make space for that person to share. There will be challenges you need to work through together and compromises to be made, not because you feel guilty or think you *have* to, but because you want the other person to be happy and you want the relationship not just to survive but to thrive. And if you've truly found your soul mate, these are the lessons you were intended to learn from each other.

Sexual Intimacy— the Ultimate Union of Soul Mates

Sex without emotional intimacy is nothing more than satisfying an urge or scratching an itch. But sex can also be the ultimate expression of intimacy, an emotional union, the reinforcement of a spiritual bond between two people.

Seduction takes place in the mind, and falling in love is a beautiful emotional experience that gives higher meaning to the physical fulfillment of desire. When it comes from the heart, it's the ultimate form of communication and connection.

Sexual energy is one of our most powerful energies for creating health.

—Christiane Northrup, M.D.

To achieve that level of meaning, however, a sexual relationship has to be part of a relationship, meaning that there is a bonding between two people that fulfills both of them on the soul level as well as the physical level. Just because you're attracted to someone physically doesn't mean there's a spiritual connection. That's why we talk about soul mates and cell mates. It's certainly possible to have sex with a cell mate, but that's really nothing more than another form of bondage. It's not the same thing as the bonding that occurs when there's a connection from the heart. I've found that very often, when I tell a client that she is going to meet a soul mate, and I describe that person, the client is taken aback because she already "knows" that person, has actually seen him in her dreams. When we make that connection from the heart, we don't have to force the relationship because it was meant to happen.

In fact, if you have to force a relationship, it probably means that it wasn't meant to happen. Pam, my client, had been in a relationship with Jack for fourteen years. When I spoke with her, she said she was determined that he marry her—not because she was so in love and wanted to be married to him but because, as she put it, after all that time she believed he *should* marry her. I explained to her that this was no way to approach a marriage and that she needed to understand that it simply wasn't destined to be. She could probably insist that Jack marry her, but in the long term the marriage wouldn't be a happy one, even if it satisfied her ego in the short term.

But the opposite is also true: we can't use sexual attraction as an excuse for walking away from commitment, as one of my clients did when she reconnected with an old college lover. Jessica walked away from a comfortable life with her husband and family to be with someone whom she thought was a soul mate but who turned out to be nothing more than a sex mate. In the end, she destroyed her life for someone she thought she knew but who was, in fact, nothing more than a wishful creation of her own mind. She didn't really know him at all, and he turned out to be abusive, irresponsible, and nothing like the white knight she'd imagined him to be.

Work It Out Together

I like to tell people that you need to get in shape for a sexual relationship. I believe that literally working out with your partner is a way to strengthen the bond between you. Neurochemically, it gets the feel-good endorphins flowing through your system, and emotionally, it boosts your self-esteem. Feeling good about yourself is an important component of being able to give pleasure to another person—which is the basis for a healthy sexual relationship.

Create a Seductive Environment

➢ Use music to create a mood that stimulates sexual energy.

➢ Laugh together to relieve any lingering anxiety.

➢ Light scented candles.

➢ Touch each other.

➢ Don't be afraid to indulge your fantasies.

TANTRIC SEXUALITY

Too often in Western society, sexuality is looked upon as an indulgence of our basest animal instincts. We are told that in order to perfect our emotional and spiritual selves we need to control and deny our physical selves. Asceticism is associated with virtue; sexuality is associated with sin.

Many Eastern cultures, however, have long been much more attuned to the body/mind connection than we are. One expression of this connection is the practice of Tantric sexuality. Tantra, which originated in India more than six thousand years ago, looks upon sex in its highest form as a way to experience spiritual enlightenment.

Sex as a Spiritual Practice

Of course, people generally think about the physical satisfaction they derive from a healthy and fulfilling sexual relationship. But when the physical satisfaction is experienced as an expression of the joining of two people's *chi*, or life force, it takes on a spiritual dimension.

Different people's energies have different frequencies, and when we meet someone to whom we're immediately attracted, it's because our spiritual and sexual energies are on the same frequency as his or hers. The problem is that many people get so caught up in the sexual energy that they to ignore the spiritual component—which is actually deeper and more meaningful, even though the sexual may seem to be more powerful at first.

When you're spiritually connected to your sexual partner, you will both be experiencing a higher level of yourselves. You'll be raising both your body and your mind to a state of higher awareness, and you'll be opening each other's center of energy, or chakra, related to the heart.

To give of yourself so totally and unconditionally takes courage; you can't approach it from a place of fear. One client I remember came to me because she was finding it impossible to form a strong, deep connection with a man. She told me that she came from a "perfect" family—her mother was perfect, her father was perfect, and they had a perfect relationship. Because of this perception, she was terrified that she, and whomever she found as a partner, wouldn't be able to live up to that degree of perfection. She didn't have the courage to give herself completely to another person because she didn't have enough confidence that her self would be good enough.

A Word to the Wise

Love is a spiritual test. The more you
practice, the better you do.

Let Go of Your Cell Mates

Making room for a soul mate can sometimes require letting go of a cell mate. Have you ever had a top dresser drawer that gets so filled up with junk that you have to paw through unmatched socks, single earrings, and extra buttons from clothing you no longer own just to get to the one thing you're looking for? If this scenario sounds familiar to you, you'll understand that you can also accumulate a lot of old, useless, or toxic relationships that prevent you from getting to the one person you want or need to find.

If you've chosen to bring these cell mates into your life you can now choose to let them go. Do you hate getting up and going to work every day because the people in your office or the person you work for is always making you feel bad about yourself? Then do something about it—ask for a transfer, look for another job, let your boss or your coworkers know that you will no longer allow them to put you down. Do you have a friend who's sucking you dry instead of filling you up? Just because you've known her since second grade doesn't mean you have to stay handcuffed to her for life. Even—or especially—if it's a lover or life partner who is limiting your life, you can cut the cord that's holding you down.

If your cell mate is a relative, it may be more difficult, but it can be done. Author Mordecai Siegal has wisely said, "Acquiring a dog may be the only opportunity a human ever has to choose a relative." That doesn't mean, however, that just because someone is a relative you need to allow him or her to keep bringing negativity into your life. No one gets to be your permanent cell mate simply by right of birth!

Not so long ago, a good friend of mine found herself in an extremely toxic relationship with her siblings. Her father had serious emphysema and her mother had Alzheimer's disease. My friend had been taking care of both her parents with virtually no help at all from any of her three sisters. After their dad died, however, the sisters sued her for custody of their mother. Luckily, the judge denied their petition for custody, but by that point my friend was so distraught and under so much stress that she was really at the end of her rope. Finally, her husband sat her down and said, "Look what they're doing to you! What this is all about is greed and guilt." It was at that point that my friend realized she simply had to cut herself off from her siblings in order to save herself.

In another instance a gentleman came to see me because the conflicts he was having with his younger brother were so debilitating that they had actually affected his physical health. The two men had been in business together, and my client's brother, through mismanagement and plain, outright greed, had driven them into bankruptcy. My client was furious, but the more we talked, the clearer it became that his anger was misdirected. It seems that before her death, his mother had made him promise to always take care of his baby brother. Although he was mad at his brother for his bad behavior, he was also mad at his mother for having extracted that promise. What I helped him to understand was that his mother hadn't meant him to put up with his brother's bad behavior. To make peace with himself, my client needed to forgive his mother and let go of his brother—no matter what he had promised.

I would hope that the majority of those close to you are soul mates, but if someone is not, and that person is dragging you down, whether it's a sibling or a parent, you simply have to stand back and refuse to be a victim. You need to do that because by keeping any cell mate close you are absorbing his or her bad energy. By removing yourself from his or her energy field, you will take back your power and free yourself. Depending upon the particular situation, the distance you create may be physical or it may be emotional. If you can't physically separate yourself from a family member, you can still refuse to allow him or her to control your emotions.

Before you do that, however, it's important that you forgive the other person. Remember that everyone is contending with his or her own issues, and that other people's psychological, emotional, and spiritual baggage are what's causing them to behave the way they do. In fact, a relative may have been put in your path just so you can learn how to step away from whatever he or she is sending your way. If you're not lucky enough to have someone like my friend's husband to sit you down and set you straight, you may need to consult a therapist who can help you get to the point where you are able to distance yourself from a toxic relative.

Gather Your Soul Mates around You

When you find a soul mate, as I've said, you'll know what he or she is thinking, you'll have the same likes and dislikes, you'll be totally comfortable in the relationship and feel as if you'd known each other for years, even if you've just met. And if you haven't seen each other in years, the bond will still hold. Is there an old friend with whom you've lost touch but whom you still think of fondly? Pick up the phone and make a call; if it's a soul mate you're calling, he or she has probably been thinking of you, too.

Having negative people in your life draws out the negativity in you, which then just attracts more of the same. It's a vicious cycle. Once you break the cycle, however, you'll have made room for your positive energy to flow. Reinforce that good energy by spending more time with your soul mates and you'll find that the flickering flame grows stronger and you begin to draw in more and more positive people.

A Checklist for Filling Your Treasure Chest with Soul Mates

✓ *Make a list of the qualities you seek in a soul mate and don't be afraid to ask for what you want.*

✓ *Put reminders of the person you want to bring into your life in your treasure chest.*

✓ *Affirm your intentions on paper and put them away someplace safe.*

✓ *Make an honest assessment of your relationships with the people in your life right now.*

✓ *Look for negative patterns in your relationships and affirm your intention to change them.*

✓ *Make peace with the past so that it doesn't continue to negatively impact your present.*

✓ *Let go of any cell mates you may have been harboring in your life.*

✓ *Gather your soul mates around you and appreciate what they give you.*

✓ *Discover sex as a spiritual experience.*

MAKE SURE YOUR HOME IS YOUR CASTLE

Your home is, in and of itself, a kind of treasure chest. It's the place where you gather your most precious possessions, so the way you design and maintain not only your dwelling but everything that dwells within it can either enhance or inhibit your physical, emotional, and spiritual well-being.

Your home is, of course, a physical space, but there may be more in that space than meets the eye. And what you *can't* see may be taking up more room than you realize. You can't see negative or positive energy, but the space itself, along with everything in it, is constantly giving off vibrations that impact your life. When those vibrations are good, you'll be the king or queen of your castle; when they're bad, you may be living like a prisoner in a dungeon (even if it's bright and

> *He is the happiest, be he king or peasant, who finds peace in his home.*
>
> **—Johann Wolfgang von Goethe**

sunny). Luckily, we all have the ability to make the changes that will enhance our living spaces and thus our lives. Therefore, if you are feeling less than satisfied with the way your life is going, your home is one place where you can begin to create the changes that will help you become the person you most want to be.

Is Your Home Your Palace or Your Prison?

My home, like yours, is not only my place of refuge and renewal but also the place where I gather the people I treasure most—my immediate family as well as my family of friends and supporters. Home is the place where we all should feel safest and most comfortable.

It took more than ten years before I found the home where I now live with my family, and where my wife and I believe we will be comfortable living the rest of our lives. The first time you walk into a house (or an apartment), you can feel whether it's a happy house or a sad house. I like to say that the house speaks to you. As you walk from room to room, you'll get a sense, almost at once, of whether or not it's a place you want to be. Pay attention to what you're feeling; don't try to rationalize away what your gut—your inherent sixth sense—is trying to tell you.

When my wife and I were moving, I wanted to be sure our new home would feel right, and I can't tell you how many houses I walked through before finding this one. I liked it immediately because it was old and traditional in style. It is on the site of what was originally a stable and is known as a "Yule colonial" after the architect who built it. I loved the fact that there are big wooden barn beams and a large stone fireplace in the living room. Later I found out that these were the builder's signature architectural elements and represented strength, unity, and prosperity to him. I also loved the fact that the house is set well back from the road and surrounded by stately old trees that offer a lot of privacy.

The minute I walked in, I knew it was the place for us, and, as it turned out, it was the house where my brother-in-law's best friend from childhood had grown up. Since I don't really believe in coincidence, knowing that just added to my conviction that this was the place where we were somehow meant to live.

One of my clients, a single father, had a similar experience when he was looking for a home for himself and his children. As he walked into the house where he now lives, the woman who was selling it started to show him around. After a few minutes she stopped, looked him in the eye, and said, "I want you to have this house. The house is telling me you should have it." The woman's husband had recently died and she hadn't really been sure she wanted to sell. In fact, my client was the first person to look at the place once she had finally put it on the market. I truly believe that the reason she said that to my client was that the house, which still retained the energy of her late husband, was speaking to her. And my client later told me that he, too, had known the minute he walked in that this would be his new home. Both of them had felt positive vibes that were coming from the energy in that house, just as I did when I walked into the house where we now live.

Out with the Old, in with the New

I believe that the most important thing you can do, whether you're moving into a new home or changing the energy in the place you already live, is to be sure that it's cleared of any lingering negativity. Is the energy of previous tenants/owners still hanging around? Was it the scene of something bad or sad? No matter; you can shift that old energy to create a fresh start for yourself and your home.

As it happened, the previous owner of our home (my brother-in-law's friend's father) had died there, and the first thing I wanted to do after we bought it was to be certain that there was no lingering negativity either from his death or from the spirits of the original owners. So I performed a little ritual. I lit a pure white candle, sat in each room (it's a big house, so this took some time!), and honored the dead by introducing myself, letting them know that we loved the house, and in effect asking their permission to move in and make it our own. My intention was to ensure that their energy would be in harmony with our own, that they would welcome us into their space.

Interestingly, the grandson of the original owner had come by with a picture of what the house looked like when his grandparents lived there. He asked if he could have the bench that appeared in the photo and was still standing outside the house. Of course I gave it to him; it was a way for him to connect with his own past. Then, during my ritual, I honored his grandfather by letting him know what I had done, and I asked him to give his blessing to our being in the house.

When you're planting, you don't throw out all the old, depleted soil, but you do add new, healthy soil that's full of nutrients so that your plants will grow and thrive. That's not so different from what you need to do in your home. Let those in the spirit world know that you're bringing your own energy in and that you want to make peace and live in harmony with them.

Making peace with the past—and making sure that whoever or whatever is lingering in your home will make peace with you as well—is particularly important if you are making renovations, as we were. When you make major changes to a home where spirits reside, the renovations are disturbing to them.

Recently we've been hearing about essentially wild animals, from coyotes to bears, coming into residential areas. That's because we humans have encroached on their turf, and from the animals' point of view we've been pushing them out of the place where they rightfully belong. It's the same with those in the world of spirit—when we move in, we're invading their space.

Therefore, you want to show respect to those spirits and, at the same time, let them know that you are now making this home your own. By doing that you are merging the energy of the spirit world with that of the living world. If you fail to make that connection, you may be disturbed by the spirits whose peace and quiet you've disrupted by your presence in their space.

When I was asked by the producers of a television program to visit a home in Connecticut and find out why the new owners were so uncomfortable, I could tell the minute I walked in the door that there were too many conflicting and confusing energies occupying the same space. The problem was that there had been many additions and renovations to what was originally a nineteenth-century colonial-style home, and the modern decking and additions were not in harmony with the original building. My advice to the owners was that they do whatever they could to make the newer parts of the house more compatible with the old so that the older energies could live more peacefully and compatibly with the new. If the old energy in your physical space does not flow in harmony with the new, it will become stagnant, and you will not thrive in that place.

——— *A Word to the Wise* ———

The more you know about those who have lived in your home before you, the better able you will be to merge your worlds emotionally and spiritually.

Create a Ritual That's Meaningful to You

In Thailand, on the solar New Year, the people throw water on one another to symbolize tossing out all the bad luck of the previous year and looking forward to good times to come. On Rosh Hashanah, the Jewish New Year, it is customary to throw bread into running water such as a river or stream to symbolize the casting away of sins in preparation for a fresh start. In the book of Luke, John the Baptist prophesizes that when Jesus comes, "He will baptize you with the Holy Spirit and with fire." In Iran, children run through the streets banging pots to symbolize beating out the last, unlucky Wednesday of the year. In Tibetan Buddhism, the sound of a bell is considered to represent the sound of the Buddha's voice, and bell ringing is a way to let evil spirits know that they are not welcome in a consecrated place.

I have a Tibetan bell given to me by a monk that I sometimes use when I'm asked to clear a space of unwanted spirits. I also use a ritual called smudging, which involves burning sage and cupping the smoke in my hands to waft it across the space as a way to cleanse it.

Think about the kind of ritual you would like to perform as a way to cleanse and sanctify your own living space. You can sprinkle the rooms with holy water, if that works for you, call in a spiritual adviser, burn incense, say a prayer, burn sage, or light a candle. Just be certain that you do the ritual in every corner of your new home to rid it of any leftover negative energy and make space for your own, positive vibe.

Committing your own vibration to your living space is important if you want to have a peaceful life. One client of mine, a woman who is a successful antiques dealer, has multiple homes including a flat in London and an old farmhouse in Quogue, on the South Shore of Long Island. Because she never stays in one place very long, she was having a problem deciding what to do with the farmhouse—renovate/don't renovate, keep it/sell it. Making her decision more difficult was the fact that she never felt comfortable in that house. When she called me in, she explained that the previous owners had been involved in a bitter divorce and the husband had killed himself in the farmhouse. I told her that undoubtedly the problem was that his spirit had not found peace and was still lingering there, and that's why she wasn't feeling comfortable.

With her permission, I went through the house shaking my Tibetan bell as I shooed out the bad energy and invited good spirits in. Happily, my client was immediately more at peace in her farmhouse and ultimately decided to stay.

A Word to the Wise

Once you've cleansed your dwelling space and
shifted the energy, repeat your cleansing ritual
every few months or at least once a year to prevent
the negative clutter from collecting again.

HAVE A PAINTING PARTY

Once you've done your spiritual cleansing, it's time to give your space a good cleaning from top to bottom. Then, invite a group of friends and family to come over for a painting party. They don't have to paint the whole house—this is not about redecorating on the cheap, and you probably wouldn't want them to anyway—but spending a few hours painting just one room with a group of people you care about, and who care about you, is a symbolic way to bring in the love and abundance you want and need to thrive in your home.

Old or New, It's the Energy That Matters

Many people ask me whether it would be better to move into a brand-new home so that there won't be any potentially disruptive spirits in residence. But whether the building is old or new, it can be filled with either a positive or a negative vibe. When I was on the *Today* show, for example, I was asked to go to One if by Land, Two if by Sea, an extremely long-lived and successful New York City restaurant situated in an eighteenth-century carriage house in the West Village that had once been owned and operated by Aaron Burr. Local lore has it that Burr's ghost and the ghost of his daughter, Theodosia, now haunt the space and that Theo-dosia sometimes removes the earrings of ladies sitting at the bar. All that may be so, but what I felt as soon as I walked in was that this place had always been associated with joy and creativity. Even though it was filled with spirits from the past, those spirits were working in harmony with the current owners to ensure the restaurant's success.

That, of course, isn't always the case. You probably know about cer-tain locations in your area that seem to be cursed. Business after busi-ness keeps closing until finally, one day, for no apparent reason, one succeeds and thrives. I believe that's because the new tenant has finally been able to replace the old negativity with his own positive vibration.

That said, however, even new buildings have either positive or neg-ative energy that comes from the ground on which they stand. I know this because I've seen it over and over again in my work. One client who had moved into a beautiful new development just outside Atlanta simply couldn't understand why she was suddenly having such terrible headaches. After going to the doctor and consulting with mold experts and several environmental agencies to eliminate the possibility that some kind of toxic substance was causing her problem, she called me. Although her house was brand new and totally contemporary, it was built on land with a long history of its own. I recommended that my cli-ent go to the local town hall and find out what she could about the his-tory of the place where she was living. After she'd done her research, she called me back saying that she'd been amazed to discover that her development was located on the site of a minor Civil War skirmish and that soldiers who had fallen in that battle had been buried quickly, right on the spot where she was now living, with little ceremony and nothing to mark their graves. Once she told me that, I had a pretty good idea what was responsible for the pain in her head.

Since my client was a member of the local parish, I suggested that she explain her problem to her clergyman and ask him to bless the house in order to change its energy. Once he did that, her headaches were gone, along with the negativity. She declared that it was nothing short of a miracle, but I know it was really a matter of clearing psychic clutter from her building site.

In another instance, a friend asked me to go to the home of a local doctor who had recently built and moved into a beautiful new home; he was hoping I could find out why his children were regularly being awakened by nightmares. In this case the doctor's home had been built on the foundation of an earlier house that had burned to the ground. The previous tenant was an alcoholic who, when he was drunk, regularly beat his children. When I went down to the basement of the doctor's house, I could easily see the old foundation, and I told him that, because he hadn't cleared the space before he rebuilt, his children were now reliving in their dreams what had occurred there before. Although the doctor was skeptical, he allowed me to perform a cleansing ritual.

I went from room to room burning white sage, sprinkling holy water, saying prayers, and generally making sure that I banished the negativity left by the previous tenant. I'm happy to say that the doctor's children are now sleeping peacefully in their beds, and the doctor himself is a lot less skeptical than he was.

And, finally, there was the woman who called me in because, ever since she had moved into her Manhattan brownstone, she had found herself engaging in uncharacteristically unhealthy behaviors. She had given up smoking years before but had gone back to her cigarette habit, she was becoming increasingly reclusive, and she had even caught herself neglecting to bathe. She was beginning to feel that some kind of alien being had taken up residence in her mind and body. When I went to her house, I made contact with the source of her problem, the previous resident who had been seriously depressed and had ultimately committed suicide. His spirit was such a strong presence that his lingering energy was actually affecting my client's mental attitude and personal habits. I was able to convince him that he no longer belonged there and persuade him to move on to another level and leave her alone.

So, as I always tell my clients, if you're about to move, it's important to find out as much about the history of your potential new living space as you can. To do that you need to become an investigative reporter:

> Ask the neighbors about the people who used to live there. Were they happy? Did anyone die there? Do the neighbors know why they moved?

➢ Ask the current tenants, if they're still in residence, why they're moving. What you really want to know is if there's anything about the house that's bothering them.

➢ Ask the landlord or real estate agent how the place came to be on the market. Since it's his or her job to sell or rent the property, you may not get a lot of information, but it can't hurt to ask.

➢ Go to the local bureau of records and find out who lived there before you.

➢ Go to the local library and see if there were any newspaper articles mentioning the address. If so, you may be able to find out more about events that took place there in the past. You might want to think twice about moving into a home that was the scene of a murder or a suicide. But maybe you'll find that it was a home filled with happy celebrations.

➢ Find out what was on the land before your house was built. Moving into a home built over what was previously a cemetery may provide you with roommates you'd rather not have.

Even if you've fallen in love with the place, or if you already live there and you either can't or don't want to move, you still don't have to resign yourself to living with someone else's negativity forever. You can perform a cleansing ritual to make peace with the past and so ensure that you have more peace in the present.

Once you've done that, make a deep personal commitment to yourself to keep the positive energy flowing.

—————— *A Word to the Wise* ——————

Negativity is like trash that accumulates in the soul.

What's inside Your Home Is Also Positive or Negative

You don't live alone—even if you think you do. You also live with the energy of your relationships, both past and present. Have you brought people into your home in the past whom you'd rather not have hanging around in the present? Think about it—are there former friends or lovers who may be physically gone but whose negativity is still cluttering up your home?

You don't want to wind up in a situation like that of my client Miriam, who had been in a long-term, live-in situation with a domineering, controlling man. Miriam is an extremely attractive, competent, and intelligent woman who insisted that she very much wanted to start over with someone new, but every time she met a potential new partner, the relationship would somehow unravel. Miriam had no idea why this was

PROTECT THE ENTRY TO
YOUR HOME FROM NEGATIVITY

People of the Jewish faith have, since ancient times, marked the entrance to their residence by affixing a mezuzah (a small case containing the words to one of the foundational Hebrew prayers) to the doorway. The ancients believed that the mezuzah had protective powers. It is written that the great Rabbi Yehuda HaNasi once received the gift of a precious pearl from the Parthian king and, in return, sent the king a beautiful mezuzah. The king, however, was outraged by the gift, telling the rabbi, "You have insulted me! I sent you a precious gift, and you reciprocate with a trifle of no value." In response, Rabbi Yehuda said, "The gift you sent me is so valuable that it will have to be guarded carefully. But the gift I gave you will guard you, even when you are asleep and even when you travel!"

You, too, can protect your home with an amulet or symbol that is meaningful to you. It might have a particular religious significance or its significance could be purely personal. The important thing is that it draws the positive into your home and your life.

I have an octagonal Chinese Bagua mirror hanging in the entrance to my home. The eight sides of the mirror reflect the eight compass points of the feng shui map (more about feng shui in a minute), and the mirror refracts and redirects negative energy that tries to enter my home.

happening, but she did recognize that it seemed to be a pattern for her. When she came to consult me, I advised her that her former lover was somehow continuing to control her life. She protested that she was well and truly over him, but I knew that even if she consciously believed that, there was something more going on. I kept urging her to look around, both internally and externally, to try to uncover whatever it was she'd been missing. It took her a full two years, but eventually, when she was cleaning out her closet one day, she realized that there were a number of the former lover's belongings stuck away in a box on a high shelf. By holding on to his things, even though she didn't realize it, she was actually keeping him around. When she finally disposed of his stuff, she also rid herself of his control. Once she'd made a few other changes in her environment, she was able to move on and meet a new man. (Yet another reason why it's a good idea to clean out your closets on a regular basis.)

Also, think about your relationships with those who have passed, particularly if they are family members. Do you have unfinished business that's keeping you from grieving their loss and getting on with your own life? Do you have photographs or other mementos of them in your home? If you're still harboring negative feelings about something either you or the deceased did or didn't do in relation to the other, now is the time to make peace with the past. Forgive your loved one and/or forgive yourself.

AN EXERCISE IN FORGIVENESS

In the previous chapter we talked about forgiving yourself for past mistakes. Now it's important to understand that your friends and loved ones in the spirit world also want you to be at peace. One thing almost all my clients worry about is whether a loved one who has died is angry with them. What I tell these people is that those in spirit want to forgive and forget and that when you're at peace with them, they too will be more peaceful.

To do this, I suggest that you first write down both the positive and negative aspects of your relationship with this person. Once you've done that, create an exercise in forgiveness: Find a photo or something that belonged to the deceased. Hold it in front of you and say the words you weren't able to say when he or she was alive. Yell if you want, talk to the deceased, get it all out, and release the negative feelings you've been harboring. Release your anger and then offer your forgiveness. By saying those words of forgiveness you'll be doing something loving and positive for yourself as well as for the person you're forgiving.

Once you've been able to forgive, honor the dead by creating a place in your home to keep his or her memory. You can put photos or other mementos in a special place to create a kind of shrine. Or, like one of my clients who placed a hope chest she'd received from her grandmother in her new hallway, you can bring in a piece of furniture or an accessory that belonged to the person who has passed. Just be sure when you do this that you've truly made peace with the past so that the new energy you create is loving and positive.

The only way to peace is forgiveness.

—Pope John Paul II

--- A Word to the Wise ---

It's important to honor your ancestors. Bringing in a piece of furniture or an object you've inherited from a loved one not only honors the person who has passed but also brings the warmth of happy memories into your home.

Are There Spirits in Your Home You Don't Know About?

Beyond the energy of your past relationships, you may also be living with the energy of people you've never met that's clinging to the objects in your home. Whether they're feeling ill at ease or just plain ill, people often call me in to determine why they seem to be so uncomfortable emotionally or physically in their home. When I get there, I almost always feel the same kind of negativity they're experiencing. When I contact someone in the spirit world, I can usually tell whether he or she died from a heart problem, a lung problem, or even some kind of blow to the head, and the feelings I get when I walk into someone's home aren't really very different from that. Here's an example.

One woman who had recently moved into a Manhattan townhouse asked me to figure out why her young son—who had always been perfectly healthy—was suddenly having asthma attacks for no reason the doctors could determine. As soon as I walked into her living room, I too began to feel a heaviness in my chest and to have difficulty taking a deep breath. When I began to question the woman about the history of her townhouse, she told me that the previous owner had died of lung cancer and, furthermore, that the living room sofa on which her son often sat while he was watching television had actually belonged to him. Sometimes I really wonder what people could be thinking! Of course that sofa was the cause of her son's breathing problems.

I told my client that—as often happens when someone dies after a long illness—the previous owner's spirit had remained earthbound, and his energy was still clinging to the sofa. Sometimes, depending upon the circumstances of the death, the person's spirit doesn't realize he or she is dead. This is particularly true when the death is sudden or accidental, but it can also happen when someone has been lingering for a period of time between life and death and doesn't realize when he or she has passed over.

As a psychic, I was able to let the spirit know he no longer belonged there and ask him politely to leave. I told my client that she could keep the sofa if she really wanted to, but she would have to do something to shift its energy and make it her own. She could do that by reupholstering it in a different fabric or just by putting new throw pillows on it. Since it was a good, costly piece of furniture, she decided to reupholster it. Sure enough, once she made the change, her son's breathing problems disappeared almost immediately.

Change the Energy and Make It Your Own

When you walk through the door of your home after a long and possibly stressful day, how do you feel? You should feel relaxed, protected, lighter, and more energetic. If you're feeling tense, tired, restless, or overwhelmed, you need to pay attention to where those negative feelings might be coming from so that you can make the necessary changes. It usually isn't difficult to change the negative energy in a room, but—like my client with the sofa—you have to discover the energy's source before you can begin to change it. You don't need a psychic to do that. Just ask yourself these questions:

- Do you have furniture or objects in your home that have been handed down or given to you? If so, the previous owner's energy may still be clinging to the object.

- If an item was inherited, how do you feel about the person who left it to you? If you didn't like your aunt Alma, her coffee table may be making you uncomfortable. Do the forgiveness ritual described on page 97. You might want to sit on her sofa and, if you have one, hold a photograph of your aunt or some object that belonged to her and tell her that you want to make peace. Then, change the appearance of that coffee table—paint it, replace the top, refinish it. By doing that, you'll be changing its energy at the same time you honor and create harmony with your aunt.

- Do you have secondhand furniture or other objects that were not brand new when you acquired them? Since you don't know where your secondhand lamp or antique rug came from, it would be best to ensure that it isn't harboring negative energy from its previous owner(s). You can do that simply enough by placing your own furniture on the rug or changing the lampshade. Make a little ritual of it. You can address the spirits whose energy these objects are harboring and let them know that you respect and appreciate what they've left behind but that they now need to let go of those things once and for all.

——— *A Word to the Wise* ———

If you're buying an antique, be sure that you feel comfortable with it before you bring it into your home. Inanimate objects send out the vibrations of those who have owned them, and if you pay attention you will be able to sense whether those vibes are positive or negative for you.

Leave Your Own Stuff Behind

Sometimes it's our own negativity that's dragging us down. Just because we're moving doesn't mean that we aren't carrying our problems with us. Our subconscious mind tends to cling to our disappointments—in love, with family, in our career—so what we need to do is clear our own negative thoughts and promise ourselves that they will no longer have a place in our home or our life. We need to lighten the load by dumping whatever it is that's dragging us down—both literally and figuratively.

Throughout my time in college I had always lived in basement apartments, and I now believe that my choice of living spaces had something to do with hiding from the world and not being comfortable with my path in life. Moving into our new house was my way of making the statement that I was now proud of myself and my work and was coming out of hiding, so to speak, even though I hadn't literally lived in a basement for some time. The move occurred just when my first book was being published and as I was about to start on a second. I was also beginning to appear on radio and television and, generally speaking, stepping into myself and becoming the person I had never allowed myself to be.

Are you constantly moving from one place to another and never feeling comfortable? If, for example, you keep moving from one dark apartment to another, you're probably repeating a negative pattern and carrying your own darkness with you.

Go back to the self-assessment you did in the first chapter and ask yourself:

1. What has gone wrong in my life that is preventing me from reaching my goals?

2. Is my home reflecting my own negative energy?

Remember that our living spaces are reflections of us. Therefore, we want to make those spaces as positive, uplifting, and energizing as possible.

In addition to dumping old emotional baggage, we need to get rid of our actual physical trash. If you've been living in one place for a long time, you've probably accumulated a lot of clutter. If you're moving, leave it behind. If you're staying where you are, make it your business to go through what you've got and get rid of whatever you no longer need or want.

If you're a pack rat, it's probably because you have trouble letting go—of both physical and spiritual baggage. Perhaps you needed to surround yourself with all that stuff to protect yourself. Now's the time to let it go. Remember the old saying "One man's trash is another man's treasure"? Keep only what you truly treasure and do something good by giving the rest to charity. The goodwill you show by doing that will come back to you in positive ways.

Janice, a client who had recently lost her husband, was moving from the large house where her now-grown children had been raised into a smaller and more manageable place, but she was having a hard time because the home she was leaving held so many memories that she simply couldn't decide what to leave and what to keep. In the end, she came up with a great solution. What she took was the door where her children's and grandchildren's growth had been marked off and compared to the height of her late husband. She had to buy the new owners a replacement door, but the cost was very small when compared to the precious memories the old door held for her.

When my family moved, I wanted to be sure that we weren't holding on to anything we didn't need or that had a negative connotation. As luck (or fate) would have it, we had a major flood in our previous house shortly before we moved, so we were forced to part with many things we might

MAKE YOURSELF AT HOME

One of my clients, whom I'll call Joe, was having serious problems with his career; he was constantly moving from one job to another, but no matter what he did, he simply couldn't get ahead. The minute I walked into Joe's house and saw all the mover's boxes stacked in the hall, I knew what the problem was. He'd lived in his apartment for almost a year by that time, and the place was still full of cartons he said he hadn't had time to unpack. Those cartons were an outward expression of Joe's internal attitude toward life: he couldn't commit to anything because he assumed that everything was temporary.

When you move into a new place it's important that you unpack immediately and make it your own. Don't live out of boxes! When you keep boxes around it may mean that you really don't want to be there or that you don't plan to be there very long. Perhaps you're hanging on to old fears. Doing any of those things will inhibit your opportunities for spiritual growth and future success.

otherwise have been tempted to hold on to. Water is, of course, cleansing, and I believe that our flood created a kind of cleansing ritual for us.

A cluttered home encourages mental and emotional clutter as well. Once you clear your living space, you'll be able to think more clearly and will be more likely to see the negative patterns that may have been preventing you from becoming all you can be.

A Short Course in Psychic Feng Shui

Once you've cleared out the old stuff, it's time to bring in the new. The ancient Chinese art of feng shui is a way to make your living space not only more physically comfortable but also more emotionally and spiritually empowering. Although it is a complicated system, two of the most basic tenets of feng shui involve the use of color and the five elements (wood, water, metal, earth, and fire), both of which I've incorporated into my own home.

THE FIVE ELEMENTS

Each of the elements has unique properties.

Wood: Promotes creativity, motivation, inspiration, and passion.

Water: May be trickling, as in a fountain, to encourage networking, communication, professional opportunities, and wealth, or it may be running like a leaky tap or a malfunctioning toilet, which would indicate a loss of money or poor health.

Metal: A conductor of energy and, like a copper bracelet, may help to protect your health. Too much metal, on the other hand, may attract too much energy and thereby prevent a space from feeling restful and relaxing.

Earth: Associated with solidity, stability, and permanence. If a room has a lot of metal in it, an object related to earth, such as a plant, can counteract that excess energy.

Fire: Represents passion and is considered the most powerful of the elements. Too much fire impedes relaxation; too little means that your life force is weak.

THE FENG SHUI OF COLOR

Colors, like the elements, have various properties, and they are also related to the elements themselves. In addition to listing the traditional feng shui meanings of the various colors, I've also included my own personal interpretation of their significance, which may in some instances be somewhat different from the associations of the ancients.

Colors Associated with Wood

Brown: Associated with industriousness, hard work, being grounded.

To me, browns symbolize Mother Earth, and I consider them to be nurturing.

Green: Represents harmony, balance, and physical, emotional, and spiritual healing.

Green is the color of healthy grass, which I associate with abundance. Keeping a green plant near the entrance to your house will draw in abundance and healing energy. My kitchen has touches of light green, which to me signify growing good food and nurturing the soul.

Colors Associated with Water

Blue: Calming and soothing, healing and relaxing but also, because it is the color of the sea and the sky, associated with adventure and exploration. Navy blue is the color of intellect.

I think of blue as the color of expansion and associate it with manifesting one's dreams and ambitions. One of my sons loves blue, and his room is painted royal blue (a compromise between the dark blue he wanted and the lighter blue we would have preferred).

Black: Associated with money, career advancement, and power.

This is one instance where I believe cultural associations really come into play. For Asians, black is associated with the mud of the rice patties, the source of their most basic food. For us Westerners, however, it is more often associated with death and mourning. The "blackness" of black can be enlivened and balanced by adding something red or putting a living plant on or near the black object.

Colors Associated with Metal

White: Represents purity, goodness, and trustworthiness as well as poise and confidence.

For me it is also reliable, representing consistency and safety. In my own home the trim around the doors and windows is painted linen white.

Gray: Because it is neither black nor white, gray is associated with indefiniteness.

I think of gray as a negative color because I associate it with a gray day and the color of battleships. To balance the effects of gray in the same way you do black, add the vibrancy of red, orange, or purple, or the warmth and energy of bright yellow.

Colors Associated with Earth

Light yellow: Reflects nourishment and stability.

Like bright yellow (see below), I associate light yellow with the feeling of inner warmth you get on a beautiful sunny day.

Beige: Associated with neatness but also with covering up emotions.

I believe beige is a "safe" color, and I associate it with people who are emotionally constricted.

Colors Associated with Fire

Red: The color of good fortune, recognition, respect, and confidence. Red flowers attract financial security to your home.

For me it is the color of passion, of the blood that flows through the body. It attracts energy and makes it grow.

Orange: Strengthens concentration; the color of organization.

I associate orange with a refreshing glass of juice that boosts both physical and emotional health.

Purple: Boosts spiritual awareness as well as spiritual and mental healing.

Purple is about your soul energy, your higher self. People with a purple aura (see page 112, violet) are generally very spiritual and intuitive.

Pink: The color of love!

Bright yellow: Like red, an auspicious color associated with warmth and energy, health and cheerfulness. A vase of yellow flowers in the center of your home will keep you centered and balanced.

To me it is happy and sunny.

AURAS, RAINBOWS, CHAKRAS, AND THE POWER OF COLORS

Many traditions in addition to feng shui associate colors with various energy sources and states of being. Red, orange, yellow, green, blue, indigo, and violet are the seven colors of the rainbow, which are represented in the electromagnetic field visible as the aura that surrounds all living things. These colors are also related to the seven chakras, or energy sources, in the human body.

+ **Red** is related to the first chakra at the base of the spine and is connected to our grounding and physical survival.

    When I see people with a red aura I know they are fiery, passionate, sexual, and tend to live in the moment.

+ **Orange** is associated with the second chakra, at the lower back and hips, and is related to emotion and desire.

    An orange aura tells me that the person is probably an adrenaline junkie—a risk taker like a paratrooper or a Green Beret, who loves a challenge and will usually go beyond what's expected.

+ **Yellow** is associated with the third chakra, in the solar plexus, and is related to strength of will and self-esteem.

    When someone has a yellow aura he is generally content with himself and his world.

+ **Green** is associated with the fourth chakra, in the heart area, and is related to loving relationships.

When I see a green aura, I'm seeing someone who is creative and nurturing of both himself and others.

- *Blue* is associated with the fifth chakra, in the throat, and is related to clarity and communication.

  I have found that people with blue auras tend to be extremely loyal, with a strong sense of family, and very often are actors or entertainers.

- *Indigo* is associated with the sixth chakra, located in the brow or forehead, and is related to intuition or imagination—what we sometimes refer to as the sixth sense.

  Indigo is what I think of as purple, which is indicative of someone who is deeply spiritual and sensitive.

- *Violet* is associated with the seventh chakra, located at the top of the head, and is related to the intellect and awareness.

  Very often, I find people with violet in their aura are mediums or do some kind of healing work.

Most people are instinctively drawn to or prefer the colors that represent their strongest characteristics, but it's important to bring other colors into your environment in order to enhance the qualities that may be less developed and balance those that are dominant. If, for example, you are predominantly a red person, bringing in some indigo or purple will encourage you to become more spiritual, and violet will balance your physicality with an increase of intellectual energy.

Using Feng Shui to Enhance
Your Living Space and Your Life

I incorporated my own psychic feng shui into my home, and you too can use elements of feng shui to ensure that your living space enhances and creates balance in every aspect of your life.

FIND A SPACE FOR SPIRITUAL CONNECTION

This is your sacred space, where you say your prayers or practice your yoga or do your meditation. It's where you go to ask for guidance. It's where you give thanks for your blessings and acknowledge the helpful people in your life. To enhance the energy of this space you might light a candle, burn incense, or bring in the aromas of sandalwood, frankincense, or sage. Bring in objects that represent the blessings in your life, including photos of those to whom you wish to give honor and recognition.

My own home has several bedrooms, so I painted one purple (for spiritual awareness and healing), displayed meaningful gifts people had given me over the years, and made it the place where I do my physical exercise and my meditation for spiritual revitalization. When I first get up in the morning, I go into my purple room and think about what I want and don't want in my world that day. I deal with my fears and do my morning cleanse.

Very often, if my day has involved working with people who are in anguish spiritually or emotionally, some of that energy has been transferred to me, and although I do my best to wash it away before I go home (see page 21), sometimes there are unhappy spirits who visit and disturb me during the night. So, in the morning, I say a prayer, thank the higher powers for what I've been given, and release any left-over stress that may be causing tension in my neck and back or gastro-intestinal problems.

CREATE A CORNER FOR PROSPERITY AND ABUNDANCE

When we think of abundance we think of the fruits of the earth, the colors brown and green, and vibrant growth. To enhance your own abundant growth you might purchase a lucky bamboo plant. Bamboo is a totally renewable resource; if you cut it down, it grows right back. Bamboo plants with eight stalks are considered to bring wealth and abundance.

In our home, the library already had wood shelves. We added plants to make it our special place of abundance.

MAKE A PLACE FOR FAME

This is the place where you might want to use vibrant reds, bright lights, and crystal chandeliers. This is where you will keep your own light burning bright. If you have a fireplace, that would be the spot to create your fame corner.

YOUR OFFICE IS ALSO
A PERSONAL SPACE

According to the *New York Times*, the average American spends forty-five hours a week at work (although many of us seem to spend a lot more). That's a lot of office time, so you need to be as aware of what you're bringing into your office as you are of what's in your home. Your office should reflect who you are in the same way your home does. To make whatever time you spend in the office as productive and positive as possible, you need to make sure that you're working in an energizing environment.

Here are a few tips for making your office a place where you flourish:

✦ Do you know who worked there before you? It's just as important to clear negative energy from your office as it is to clear it from your home.

✦ Clean out the drawers, the shelves, and the file cabinets. Pitching the previous occupant's personal belongings (or your own leftover clutter) will eliminate negative energy.

✦ Shift the energy by making the space your own. If you can't actually move or replace the furniture, bring in a photo of a loved one or another personal belonging that has positive associations for you.

✦ Bring in something you can look at that makes you feel calm and peaceful and reminds you of the greater meaning of your life.

- Create a "success" or "fame" corner in a color associated with recognition (see page 114).

- Bring in something metal to help you gain clarity and precision in your work.

- If you're moving your own things from a previous office, make certain that you leave behind anything that had a negative meaning for you.

- If you've been feeling sluggish and stagnant in your job, clean out your workplace. Go in on a weekend if you have to and just be relentless—pitch, toss, get rid of all the stuff that's been preventing the creative energy from flowing.

- Place your desk as far from the entrance as possible to draw *chi* or life force toward you rather than blocking it, and make sure that you sit facing the door so that you're inviting in more that's good and profitable, not turning your back on it!

- If your office has fluorescent light, augment or replace it with a desk lamp that has full-spectrum light, which most closely simulates natural sunshine. Cool, white fluorescent light has been banned in Germany because studies have shown that it has a negative impact on health and well-being, which in turn negatively impacts productivity.

- Bring in touches of red for increased energy, orange for concentration, purple for inspiration, and yellow to make it a happy space.

My own fame corner happens to be in my office. It's where I've hung photos of myself appearing on various television programs as well as photos of my family. On one wall, I've hung a poster with a beautiful photograph of soaring trees with fall foliage set against a blue sky and the following legend:

THE ESSENCE OF SUCCESS

Successful is the person who has lived well, laughed often and loved much, who has gained the respect of children, who leaves the world better than they found it, who has never lacked appreciation for the earth's beauty, who never failed to look for the best in others or to give the best of themselves.

By combining the poster and the photos I am reminding myself of what I've accomplished as well as what I aspire to.

Do an Emotional and Spiritual Walk-Through

Although most of my clients come to see me in my office, I am sometimes asked to go to a person's home because the family is simply uncomfortable in their surroundings and can't figure out exactly what's wrong. Now we're going to do what I do when I visit a client. We're going take a virtual tour of your home, room by room, so that you can think about what you are feeling in each one. If there is negative energy anywhere in your physical space, you will sense that negativity and not be comfortable there.

I've certainly never claimed to be a decorator, but, as I've said, people do call me into their home when they realize that some aspect of their life is not going well and they suspect that the reason may be hiding in their living space. When I get there, I look around and do basically the same thing I suggest that you do for yourself. Walk around and become aware of how you feel in each room. Think about those areas where you would like to see improvements in your life. If, for example, you're worried about your financial situation, take a look at the place where you do business or pay your bills. Is it light and airy or dark and uninviting? Is it full of clutter that's cutting off the flow of positive energy? Do you have a dying plant or a piece of equipment that is no longer working? How can you change that negative energy to create a positive (cash) flow? Too many people are inclined to just "go with the flow" and don't consider how they could make things flow so much better.

Do this for each area of your home and make the small changes that will create major changes for the better in your life.

WHAT IS THE ENERGY OF YOUR BEDROOM?

We're going to start our tour in the bedroom because that is the most intimate part of your home, the place where you replenish your spiritual and physical life force. It's the room where love is consummated and also the place where you're most vulnerable when you sleep, so it has to make you feel both emotionally open and safe. I like to call the bedroom your own personal heaven.

If you've been sleeping badly, if you feel restless when you need to rest, or if your love life has been lacking, you may need to do a bit of psychic feng shui to create more balance and allow the positive energy in your bedroom to flow freely.

Let's look around.

First of all, think about how your bed is situated. Be sure that the head (whether or not you have a headboard) is set against a wall for stability and that it isn't hidden under a shelf or a beam that would impede the flow of energy around it. (Storing things under the bed, as so many of us do, also blocks energy.) The bed should be accessible from both sides to amplify and encourage sleep and, if you're trying to bring someone into your life, to send the psychic message that you are open to sharing your bed and your life in a spiritual as well as a sexual sense.

Now, what about color? If you go back to the meaning and associations of the colors and elements, you'll see that having a bedroom filled with colors and objects associated with metal and fire might keep you up at night, while a room based on nothing but watery blue might make it hard for you to get up and get going in the morning. Think about what you are trying to enhance or encourage. A combination of pink and red would help to make you lucky in love, and a soft purple would promote spiritual and mental healing, but if you choose one or more of those fiery colors you'll need to offset them with a touch of light yellow for stability and perhaps a blue accent for relaxation. Too much fire in the bedroom could leave you tossing and turning or feeling like a kid on a sugar high.

Do you watch TV in bed? If so, you need to hide it away when it's time to go to sleep so that the electromagnetic energy it emits doesn't disturb your rest.

Finally, to constantly create new *chi*, be sure to clean out your closets on a regular basis. Do you have clothing you no longer wear and whose energy is worn out? If so, give it to charity. By doing that you'll be helping someone in need at the same time you're helping yourself.

Your bedroom is the place where you renew yourself and restore your health, so be sure that it provides you with a beautiful and harmonious environment.

IS YOUR LIVING ROOM INVITING AND INVIGORATING?

If your bedroom is intimate and private, your living room is the place where you welcome others into your life. Our living room is the only room in the house that doesn't have a television because we want to keep it a place for conversation and social gatherings.

Look at your furniture arrangement:

> Can you see the door wherever you sit?
> If the back of a piece of furniture is blocking off the energy that comes through the door, you may be feeling isolated and lonely.

WHERE DO YOU KEEP YOUR COMPUTER?

Many of us these days have some kind of home office or at least a place where we keep the computer, pay bills, and generally take care of business. Very often, when we're cramped for space, that office is carved out of a corner in the bedroom.

One dynamic young woman I know is in the fashion business and maintained a home office in a corner of her bedroom. She called me one day complaining that she was having a terrible problem getting to sleep at night. She simply couldn't turn off when it was time to wind down and give her mind a rest while her spirit was renewed. Instead ideas for new designs and thoughts about what she needed to do the next day kept swirling around in her head.

As I explained to her, the problem was that she hadn't clearly defined the boundary between her work space and her sleeping space, and that lack of physical boundary was blurring her mental boundaries as well.

When clients complain that they are restless at night or that they go to bed and wake up thinking about work, I always ask if they have a home office and where it is located. If there is no actual wall between their work space and their sleeping space, I always recommend that they find a way to differentiate between the two. You can do that as well. When you're finished working for the day, cover your computer (or close it if it's a laptop) and put up a screen around your work space to put it out of sight and out of mind. I guarantee that your nights will be more restful and, as a result, your days will be more productive.

> Is your seating arranged in a U shape to facilitate communication and connection?

If you've created a seating arrangement that discourages conversation, even though you are welcoming guests you won't be absorbing the positive energy they could otherwise be sending your way.

Here are a few other life-enhancing living room tips to consider:

> Light, bright, clear colors encourage lively social intercourse and clarity of thought. To enhance the brightness of your living room and your life, put brightly colored throw pillows on your sofa or hang a colorful piece of artwork.

> Make sure there is space not only around but also under your furniture for energy to flow freely.

> Running water, as in a small indoor fountain, will encourage communication.

> A living plant enhances stability and will help to cement and deepen relationships.

> Rounded corners allow energy to flow while pointy corners cut it off, so soften the corners of your room with a screen or a plant.

——— *A Word to the Wise* ———

Avoid artificial plants, which have no life force.
Even if you have a totally brown thumb, you can
bring in a cactus or a bamboo plant, both of
which are alive and require almost no care.

DECLUTTER YOUR KITCHEN

Just as I don't claim to be a decorator, I certainly know I'm not a cook (and my family would definitely agree), but I do know that the one place in your home that really needs to function efficiently is your kitchen. The kitchen, according to feng shui, is the soul of your home. It should be a place of abundance, where you're putting "wealth" into your body. And yet this is also the place where clutter and old, stale energy can accumulate most easily. We all tend to ignore half-used jars of stuff or forgotten leftovers in the refrigerator. When we replace a damaged or broken piece of equipment, we often hang on to the old one just in case. All this leftover junk creates psychic clutter, which prevents the room where we prepare the food that sustains our life from being as life-enhancing as it could and should be. I even suggest that if you bring in food from the deli, Chinese restaurant, or pizzeria, you transfer it to your own containers to minimize the negative energy that may have come in with the food.

A burner that isn't working on your stove diminishes the fire of your life force. What you need to do is keep all your equipment in good repair so that you will be cooking up prosperity.

Stainless steel appliances are metal and, therefore, protective of health, and the color white, so often associated with kitchens, connotes purity and goodness. I've already said that I have touches of green (for healing and abundance) in my kitchen, but bright yellow, associated with health, is also a good color to use in a kitchen.

Keep a tomato or strawberry plant on the kitchen windowsill for abundance.

ENHANCE NURTURING IN THE ROOM WHERE YOU DINE

Your dining room or table is where you nurture and feed not only your family but also those whom you want to bring closer and draw into your intimate circle. That's why I believe a round or oval table is the best shape to have, because it supports easy interaction among those who are sharing a meal. I also believe in having an even number of chairs to create more harmony. Lighting that does not cast shadows increases clarity. And keeping your table clear of unopened mail, old magazines, and other clutter prevents the buildup of stale, stagnant energy.

As is true in many families, my kids often do their homework at the dining room table (that's also a good way for my wife to keep an eye on them and be sure it's getting done), but we always make certain that when they're finished, they pack up their books and papers and leave the table neat and clean.

Make the place where you dine a kind of sacred space, a place to acknowledge the abundance of life with which you've been blessed. Put a single bud in a glass of water at each person's place when you dine to ensure calm and harmony at the table.

DOES YOUR BATHROOM ENCOURAGE HEALTHY RENEWAL?

Energy flow is as important here as it is in every room of your house, but whereas a tinkling fountain would create positive flow in your living room, a leaky faucet in the bathroom is a way for energy to go down the drain and be wasted. One of my clients was having a hard time holding on to her money. Every time she received a payment, some unexpected expenditure would come up and, before she knew it, the money was gone. When I went to her house to help her find out why her money was being "flushed away," as she put it, I found there was a leak in the bathroom wall that she'd been unaware of. Once the leak was fixed, her financial situation improved dramatically.

A blocked pipe, on the other hand, means that old waste matter (negative energy) is building up and making it more difficult for anything new and positive to enter the room. If you feel thwarted or blocked in some area of your life, it might be a good idea to see whether there's anything either draining or impeding the healthy energy in your bathroom.

It's no wonder that white, associated with purity, is so often the dominant color of the room most closely associated with our own purification. But since green is the color of spiritual, emotional, and physical healing and blue is soothing, calming, and relaxing, these are also important colors to include in your bathroom.

Use Light and Mirrors to Brighten and Expand Your Life

Feng shui is all about enhancing your *chi*, or life force, and one of its basic tenets is that natural light enhances that life force. The ancient Chinese may not have known about SAD (seasonal affective disorder), a syndrome that causes people to become depressed in the winter, but they certainly understood the uplifting power of sunlight. I happen to be lucky enough to live in a home that gets plenty of sunlight, but we can't all live in places where the sun always shines brightly. We can, however, make it a point to bring as much natural light as possible into our home. A simple way to do that is to be sure all your windows are clean and in good repair. Also, even though living trees represent life, having too many tall trees too close to your house can block the light that would otherwise brighten your life.

Because mirrors double the energy of whatever they reflect by creating a virtual duplicate, they play an important role in created good (or bad) feng shui. A properly placed mirror can reflect and therefore enhance the natural light coming into your home. A mirror expands space and reflects beauty, but if it is poorly placed it can also reflect a disconcerting, stressful image that may make you feel uncomfortable. You would not, for example, want to place a mirror in such a way that it reflects a desk piled with unpaid bills, nor would you want to disturb the peace and harmony of your home by hanging a mirror that reflected a busy street or your neighbor's ill-kept yard. You would, on the other hand, hang one that reflected the tranquillity and beauty of a garden or a wooded area.

Don't hang a mirror that's so small or so poorly placed that it reflects only a portion of your image, thus cutting off part of your self and making you feel less than whole. My wife and I have a mirror on the door in our bedroom. We've hung it in such a way that it is reflecting energy back toward us rather than out the door. But we also made sure that it doesn't reflect us as we sleep because, according to Chinese belief, your spirit leaves your body while you sleep and might get lost in the mirror or might become frightened by seeing its reflection and therefore disturb your sleep.

Make sure the shades in your home are pulled
up in the morning to let in the light and help to
offset any dark days you may have at work. Plants
need light to grow and thrive and so do you.

Create Harmony Throughout

When I walk through a client's home, I'm looking for flow as well as balance throughout. It's all well and good to make your bedroom the perfect place for rest, renewal, and intimate relationships, but if your living room isn't welcoming to visitors you may find yourself spending a lot of your time alone.

Once you've walked through your own home and corrected the mistakes that may have been preventing you from growing and thriving in any particular room, you also need to be sure that the energy of one room flows freely into the others and that there is a balance throughout to encourage what you feel is lacking and offset qualities that may be too dominant in yourself or your life.

A Checklist for Adding Treasures to Enhance Your Home

✓ *Do a cleansing ritual using water or herbs or whatever has personal meaning in order to get rid of your old stuff—both physical and emotional.*

✓ *Say a prayer to make peace with those who have passed and honor them in your home.*

✓ *Take a tour of your home. Determine what you can do to create more positive feng shui and keep the good energy flowing throughout.*

✓ *Think about the room(s) where you feel most peaceful. Determine why. Is it color, light, a sense of openness, a feeling of safety? Read the chapter again to determine how to enhance those qualities.*

✓ *Think about the room(s) where you feel down, depressed, or angry. Determine what it is in each room that prevents you from feeling more at peace. Read the chapter again to determine how you can clear out the negativity and get the good energy flowing.*

✓ *Think of an area in your life where you're experiencing problems. Is there something you can do in your home or office to turn around that negativity—change a color, add a living plant, create a success corner?*

BRING MORE PROSPERITY INTO YOUR LIFE

Let me start out by saying that bringing prosperity into our lives isn't all about making more money. Sure, we all desire wealth and, more importantly, the financial freedom to take care of ourselves and our loved ones. But too often we equate money with happiness; we assume that if we had enough of the first we'd automatically have more of the second. But the old adage is correct: money can't buy happiness. It can buy things, it can get you a bigger house or a fancier car, but if you believe that all you need is more money to bring you joy, peace of mind, and contentment, you're going about it all wrong.

Prosperity is a way of living and thinking, and not just money or things.

–Eric Butterworth

Positive psychologist Dr. Michael B. Frisch has found that people who are more materialistic and place high value on being rich tend to be more pessimistic and unhappy. Based on my own work and experience, I believe that's because those people are primarily dissatisfied with what they've got. They're worried that they'll never have enough and are always scheming to get more. Basically, they're thinking negatively, sending negative energy out into the world, and therefore drawing more negativity into their own lives.

Although "the power of positive thinking" has become something of a cliché, its underlying message is as powerful today as it was more than half a century ago when it was popularized by Norman Vincent Peale. Prosperity, to me, is about changing your attitude, trusting your gut feelings, and having the courage to pursue your heart's desire.

That's not to say that you shouldn't want to earn more money. The key is to be clear about *why* you want the money. Do you want to create a better life for yourself and your loved ones? Do you want to be sure that your children will have a good education, that you'll have warm clothes in the winter and the ability to take a family vacation? There's nothing wrong with wanting any of those things. Or do you want to own a closet full of expensive shoes you'll never have a chance to wear? Do you need three cars when you can only drive one at a time? Your intention, your purpose in wanting the money is what's going to determine whether you're ultimately happy or never satisfied with what you've got.

There's nothing wrong with thinking big; the big mistake is thinking greedy.

I know I'm not the first, and I will certainly not be the last person to tell you that your thoughts have energy. However, I may be breaking or at least cracking the mold when I tell you that sending out positive thoughts is just the first step. Thinking, in and of itself, isn't going to be enough to bring you the prosperity you seek. It's also going to take focus and some work on your part.

GIVE YOURSELF PERMISSION

You have the power to become whatever you most want to be. You just need to give yourself permission to step into that power. To help you do that, try this visualization.

Imagine that you are sitting on the beach and gazing out at the ocean. Look at the ebb and flow of the water. If you caught one of those outgoing tides, where would you like it to take you? Now imagine yourself swimming out with the tide as far as you want. You can do it; you can ride your dream as far as you allow it to take you. Really see it happening in your mind's eye and keep repeating the visualization until you believe it.

Stop Sweating the Small Stuff

First, go back to your self-assessment and remind yourself of what your inner voice is telling you that you really want to bring into your life (as well as what you want to let go). Take out the list you made of the things you want to change. Some of the items on your wish list are going to be easier than others to achieve. If, for example, you said "I hate my hair," just stop wasting all that negative energy and go get a haircut or color it or straighten it or curl it. Why would you spend so much time agonizing—and therefore being negative—about something you can fix so easily? If you're too afraid to change something that simple, you'll never be able to access the positive energy you need to change the things that really matter.

A lot of us spend an awful lot of time hating or worrying or simply thinking about the small stuff instead of doing anything about it. Things like that just create mental and emotional clutter. I'm not saying that your hair or your tennis game isn't important to you, but they're not the things you should be agonizing over. If you want to change your hair, go do it. If you want to improve your tennis game, take lessons. Just do it, and stop wasting all that energy you could be putting to much better use.

Get Your Priorities in Order

Albert Einstein has been quoted as saying, "Any man who can drive safely while kissing a pretty girl is simply not giving the kiss the attention it deserves." It's a scientific fact that the human mind cannot hold two conscious thoughts simultaneously.

We're all multitasking all the time. We may, for instance, be loading the dishwasher while we're talking on the phone, but that's only because we don't have to think about loading the dishwasher; we do it automatically. If we got to the point where we had to figure out how to fit in that large pot, we would momentarily stop paying attention to the conversation, and, once we got the pot situated, we'd probably say to the person on the other end of the line, "I'm sorry, I got distracted there. What were you saying?" Therefore, when it comes to making changes in our lives, we have to concentrate on one thing at a time. We need to have a plan or else we'll be trying to do too many things at once, effectively wasting a lot of energy and not doing anything very well.

Go back to your list and choose one item. This is the one you're going to focus on first. It should be important to you but not the goal that's going to be the most difficult to achieve. So, going back to the sample list on pages 24 and 25, it would be smarter to choose "I want to get a better job" than to start with "I need to become more financially secure." Why? Because if you do get a better job, you'll be on the road to becoming more financially secure. That's putting first things first, building a firm foundation for your future.

Also, once you've experienced some success, you'll begin to feel better about yourself, your capabilities, and your future. You'll be thinking more positively.

────────── *A Word to the Wise* ──────────

Use your mind like a laser beam to target
exactly what you want to achieve.

Commit to the Process

The four basic ingredients for transforming your life and getting more of what you need are:

1. Understanding your intention

2. Confirming your intention with visualizations and affirmations

3. Knowing how you will achieve your intention

4. Putting your plan into action and committing to the process

Once you've decided on your first goal, you're going to need to commit to that intention mentally and emotionally. If you continue to have doubts or fears, you won't be committing yourself totally to the process and you'll be sabotaging yourself.

One client I remember very well was a young woman who was convinced she'd never get into medical school. Janet was certainly smart enough. She'd received consistently good grades in college and she had done very well on her MCAT (Medical College Admission Test), but every time she went for an interview she performed very badly. She knew she was prepared. She just somehow didn't present herself as the competent, intelligent, and dedicated young woman she really was. When Janet came to see me, I learned that her father had always belittled her ambitions and made her feel that she wasn't good enough or smart enough to be a doctor. She had apparently internalized those feelings, and even though she didn't realize it, her subconscious beliefs were preventing her from getting what she most desired in life.

During our session together, her father, who had died a few years before, came through to me and let his daughter know that the reason he had always discouraged her was that he himself had always been afraid of taking chances, and he was afraid that if she put herself on the line she might be disappointed. Rather than putting her down, he'd actually thought he was protecting her from disappointment. Later, she spoke to her aunt who told her that her dad, who had been a medic in the Marine Corps, had wanted to go to medical school himself but had felt that he couldn't afford it because he needed to earn money right away to support his wife and infant daughter (my client).

Simply having that information was enough to change her whole attitude toward herself and her ambition. She realized that she'd been operating under a false assumption, and instead of fearing failure, she became determined to succeed and make her father proud.

We all like to hold on to old thoughts and beliefs; we just stuff them in the attic of our mind. Clean out your mental attic, open up the windows of your mind, and let the sun shine through. I realize that you may not be in a position to consult a psychic in order to overcome your doubts and fears, but if you've done your self-evaluation, you should be able to determine who or what in your past may be preventing you from building a brighter future for yourself.

When you walk around under a cloud, all hunched over and self-protective, you're sending out negative energy, and it will be a gray day. When you get out from under that cloud and emerge into the sunlight, you'll stand taller, smile at the world, and bring more light into your life. Go back to Key #3 and make sure you're surrounding yourself with brightness and the colors of prosperity.

--- *A Word to the Wise* ---

Flowers bloom in the sunlight, and so will you.

Many people, when they ask for something to come into their life, are operating from a position of negativity. They ask for what they *don't* want to happen instead of what they do. *Oh, please, don't let me lose my job. Oh, don't let me fail at this.* When you do that, you're putting out negative energy, which is unlikely to bring anything positive into your life. In fact, you're more likely to get whatever it is you're trying to avoid because that's what your mind is putting out into the universe.

———— *A Word to the Wise* ————

If you're a creature of habit, make sure that
your habits are good, positive ones.

Old habits die hard. If you were raised to be a pessimist or if pessimism is simply hardwired into your DNA, you need to take a good look at your tendencies and determine to change them. You'll probably still have doubts because that's only human. But you need to trust the process. The more you fight the process, the less likely it is to work out.

To help keep yourself positive:

➤ Avoid getting into a negative cycle of "what ifs."

➤ Surround yourself with people who support your dreams and ambitions.

> Read what you can about successful people to keep your mind focused on success.

> Draw a detailed mental picture of how you see yourself once you've achieved your goal.

Try "Seeing" with Your Mind's Eye

Most of our lives we walk around looking everywhere but inward. On a daily basis, that's a good thing because it prevents us from walking into walls or getting hit by a car. When we're trying to achieve a goal, however, what we need to do is quiet our mind, shut out all the distracting noise coming at us, and try to "see" our success with our mind's eye.

First you need to be absolutely clear about what your goal is. Then, every morning when you get up, take a few moments to visualize yourself having become what you most want to be. Picture yourself in your new surroundings. What will your workplace look like? What will you be wearing? What will you be doing? How will you feel? Be as specific as you can. Use all your senses. What will it feel like, smell like, sound like? Have you ever heard the old saying "I want it so much I can taste it"? That's the kind of energy you need to put into your visualization. You're creating this mental picture, so make sure you give yourself the starring role.

Now, affirm to yourself what it is you're seeing. Actually say the words, either out loud or to yourself.

You may not receive an Academy Award for your mental performance, but you'll receive another kind of reward. When you do this kind of visualization consistently you're training your mind to focus on success. Most people don't take the time to do this, but the better you can see what you desire in your mind's eye the more likely you will be to create it for yourself. Do it over and over again, adding more details each time. Continue to edit, embellish, and polish the story you're telling yourself. Your mind has the power to change your mental images into lived reality. If you doubt me, next time you're in your car and looking for a parking space, really concentrate on seeing a space open up in your mind. It works for me almost every time, and I guarantee that it will work for you too.

The key is that while you're doing your visualization, you really have to believe it. Your thoughts carry the power of your intention. You need to affirm that you are willing to open your mind and set aside your fears. There's nothing wrong with admitting that this is a bit frightening, but you need to state (to yourself) that you're going to go ahead with it even though you're afraid because you *know* that it's going to work for you.

What the mind can conceive and believe the mind can achieve.

—Napoleon Hill

You can't just be saying, okay, Jeffrey told me to do this, so I'm going to try it, but I really don't believe it's going to work. If that's your intention, it's not going to work, so you need to ask yourself why you don't believe it. Do you think you don't deserve it? Do you think you're just unlucky? Are you afraid that if you get what you want it still won't make you happy? Maybe you really don't know what you want. Whatever the reason, if you don't really believe you can achieve it, you'll be looking for excuses instead of working toward your goal. Therefore, you need to change those negative thoughts and beliefs.

I suggest that you begin to think of the prosperity you want to bring into your life as an unlimited credit line that's always available to you from the universal bank.

Let's say, for example, you are an independent contractor who works from home and your intention is to move to a larger home so that you can have a home office. You confirm your intention by visualizing yourself in your office in your new home; you see exactly what it will look like, where you will sit, how it will be decorated, and you affirm it to yourself by repeating something like, "I have a beautiful new office where I can work much more efficiently and comfortably and where I enjoy being every day." Now you need to determine how you're going to achieve that. "I am going to use my networking strategies to get a contract for a project that will bring in X amount of money and that will also raise my profile in my field so that I continue to get more lucrative projects in the future."

Sometimes your mind is going to want to play tricks on you. Just when you're ready to put your plan into action you'll start to remember

HOW MANY QUARTERS DO YOU HAVE?

This is a visualization I do for myself on a regular basis.

Imagine that you have a quarter. Imagine putting it down and then lining up more quarters next to it; then visualize rows of quarters. Then start lining up rows of dollars, fives, tens, hundreds, and so on.

When you do this day after day, the visualization will act like a magnet bringing money to you. You will be using the power of your mind to manifest what you want to bring into your life.

a bad experience you had in the past, and you might then begin to fear that the same thing will happen again.

Let's suppose that you'd previously intended to start a home-based business but you hadn't really thought about how to bring in clients or how many clients you'd need to make your business viable. Now you're ready to try again, but you can't help feeling that because you failed the first time, your new enterprise will also be doomed to failure. If that's what you believe, it's almost certainly what's going to happen.

What you need to do then is banish your fear by reminding yourself how much you've learned from your previous experience and exactly what it is that you intend to do differently this time. You've lined up five clients and you've done your budget. You know how much you need to make to carry you through your first year, and you've put away enough of a nest egg to carry you until the first payments come in. Just because you had a bad experience in the past, that doesn't mean you won't have a good experience now and in the future. But unless you firmly set aside your creeping negativity, it could continue to prevent you from moving forward.

And remember the truth of the old adage that says you can't please all of the people all of the time. I've certainly run into clients who haven't been pleased with what I had to tell them. I've even had to deal with threats upon occasion, but I couldn't let that kind of negativity cause me to doubt myself or divert me from the path I know I was meant to follow. If you do receive negative feedback, take another good look at your plan, and if you still know in your heart that you're on the right path, don't let the negativity of others get in your way.

A Word to the Wise

By recognizing what you do have instead of dwelling on what you don't, you'll be building on something positive that will help you get closer to your goal.

COUNTERACT EACH NEGATIVE THOUGHT WITH TWO POSITIVES

The more doubt you allow to creep into your mind, the less likely you will be to achieve your intention.

It's important to be conscious of creeping negativity because it's your fears that are getting in the way of your ability to change. Once you begin to worry or doubt yourself, you'll lose your focus and begin to spiral downward. It takes self-discipline to overcome the stumbling blocks you put in your own path. Willpower is the ability to look at your own bad thoughts and overcome them. Try to catch yourself being negative, and each time a negative thought pops into your mind, refocus and counteract it with two positives.

Let's say you're on your way to an important job interview and, as you're waiting to cross the street, a car comes along and splashes mud all over your pant leg. You can either bemoan your bad luck and convince yourself that you'll never get the job because of your muddy pants, or you can go in there and say, "You're never going to believe what happened to me on my way here." Laugh it off and tell yourself that the state of your pants is not going to prevent you from getting the job because you know you're qualified and you know how to sell yourself.

Every time I'm scheduled to appear on a television program I still get nervous. On TV you only have a short time to do whatever it is you do, and I worry that this time I'm not going to make the psychic connection or that I'll misinterpret the message. To overcome my negative thought I tell myself two things: (1) You've done this before and you've always been successful, and (2) You just have to let your instincts and abilities take over and you'll be fine. With those two positive thoughts, I counteract my negativity, and so far I have always gotten it right!

Try doing this yourself. There will always be something you can't control, but you *can* control the way you perceive things. The words you say to yourself have tremendous power. Teaching yourself to think in a new way is mind-altering. Transforming your thought process will transform your reality.

I think it's interesting that we use the term "currency" to refer to money in circulation. Both "currency" and "circulation" are terms that I associate with flow—as in the flow of energy. If we allow our negativity to cut off the flow of positive energy, we'll be undermining our ability to bring more prosperity into our own lives.

Creating Change Takes Effort

Do you remember the scene in *Peter Pan* where Peter comes through the window of the Darling children's bedroom and teaches them to fly by telling them to "think happy thoughts"? The happier their thoughts, the higher they soared.

It's true that all change begins with changing the way we think, but real life isn't a fairy tale, and simply sitting on the sofa and thinking about what you want isn't going to make it happen. You need to have a plan and you need to figure out how you're going to put that plan into action.

A young guy named Craig showed up in my office one day wanting me to tell him why he kept getting passed up for promotion at his place of work. Looking at his résumé I could see that he had all the right credentials, but looking at him I didn't have to be a psychic to get to the root of his problem. Craig was a nice-looking guy, but he was dressed like a slob. His shirttail wasn't tucked in, his shoes weren't shined, and he was badly in need of a haircut. When I suggested that his grooming (or lack thereof) might be preventing his boss from seeing him as management material, Craig looked a bit embarrassed and confessed that all his life his mother had bought his clothes and told him what to wear with what. She had practically color-coded his shirts and trousers. She'd been the one to remind him to go to the barber and he'd never had to worry about shining his shoes because his mother did it for him. She'd probably thought she was being helpful, but, in fact, she was preventing him from ever learning to do things for himself, and after she died, he was totally bereft. Not only was he mourning the loss of his mother, but also he was at a loss to know how to take care of himself.

I told Craig that while he had every right to grieve for his mother, that didn't give him the right to give in to learned helplessness. My recommendation was that he go to see an image consultant. I was sure that once he felt better about how he looked, he'd feel more confident about himself. That confidence would then show up in his attitude and demeanor, and his boss would begin to look at him differently.

The point is that if you want to make a career change or move up the ladder, you need to have a plan. You need to do something to make it happen. Let's say for example that you're an accountant with a large firm and you think you want to become an independent financial planner. What is your plan? The logical first step would be to educate yourself about what a financial planner does and get the necessary certification. Instead of telling yourself it will never happen, take evening classes at the local community college while you keep your day job. Then you might use the contacts you've made throughout your accounting career to gradually begin to take on some small business accounts. Make your own financial plan to determine how much income you'll need from your new career before you can quit your job.

Wherever it is you want to go with your career, you need to concentrate on what you're going to do to get there. Are you planning to open a shop? Do your research: Which are the neighborhoods that don't already have the kind of shop you plan to open? What kind of customers are you trying to attract? Where are they shopping now? What can you offer them that other shops don't? You don't have to be a psychic to figure all this out. You just need to put some EFFORT into it. If you do that, you *will* achieve your goal.

PUT SOME EFFORT INTO IT

To help you remember what you need to do to get what you want in your life, think of the acronym EFFORT:

Energy: Put out positive energy.

Faith: Believe that it's really going to happen.

Focus: Keep your mind on your goal.

Organize: Be very specific about what you want and how you're going to get it.

Resolve: Determine to make it happen.

Tenacity: Stick with it.

——— *A Word to the Wise* ———

If you're unhappy with the way your career is going,
don't get stuck. Update your business plan to
bring in more of what it is you need to prosper.

I've already said that it's unlikely you'll find your soul mate while you're sitting at home in your bathrobe watching television, and the same is true for whatever kind of positive change you want to bring into your life. Put it out there, wish for it, think positive thoughts, *and then get out there and do what it takes to make it happen.* It takes self-discipline and willpower to stop procrastinating and start doing what you need to do. What are the steps you're going to take to start creating change? Think of those steps as a sink full of dishes. If you keep procrastinating, the dishes will never get washed. If you start to wash one at a time, eventually—sooner rather than later—all the dishes will be done.

This isn't magic, although too often we would prefer to believe that it is, because that's a lot easier than taking responsibility for our own lives. A farmer doesn't just throw a bunch of seeds into the ground and then come back a few months later and expect to find an abundant crop. He makes sure he plants the right seeds in good, fertile soil, and then he patiently nurtures and cares for them until they grow.

A Word to the Wise

Stop focusing on the problem and
start to focus on the solution.

Sometimes, of course, no matter how carefully the farmer tends his crops, something goes wrong. There may be a drought or an early flood or a late-season frost—things over which he has no control. But that doesn't mean he's going to quit, or decide that he doesn't deserve to have a healthy crop, or that he won't be successful the next year. And you're not always going to get exactly what you hoped or dreamed either. No matter how positive you are or how much effort you put into it, you will be disappointed from time to time.

Life doesn't always go just the way we want it to. Maybe you've missed or squandered a great opportunity in the past. Maybe you had a thriving business and made mistakes that caused it to fail. That doesn't mean you can't or won't succeed the next time. When something doesn't go your way, you have the tools at your disposal to get yourself back on track, figure out what you can do differently the next time, and then do it. I know it's a lot easier to sit there and complain, but complaining is just feeding your own negativity, thereby ensuring more negative outcomes in the future. Instead, sit down and figure

Have patience with all things, but chiefly have patience with yourself. Do not lose courage in considering your own imperfections but instantly set about remedying them—every day begin the task anew.

—St. Francis de Sales

THREE TRICKS FOR IMPROVING MENTAL FOCUS

The more you are able to focus your mind, the better able you will be to tap into your own mental energy. Here are three mental exercises you can practice to help increase your focus.

This first one really is a card trick. Take a deck of cards turned facedown and sit with it in your hand. Now, really concentrate on what you think the top card in the deck is, then turn it over and see if you were right. Keep trying, keep concentrating, keep focusing. Don't keep second-guessing yourself. The more you do this, the more you are able to focus the power of your mind, the more often you'll be correct.

Another trick I teach people for focusing mental energy is to sit across from another person and put your hands up so that your palms are flat against his. Now sit quietly and focus on feeling the energy that is coming through his hands. As you sit and concentrate you will begin to feel it.

A third exercise is to find an object such as a candle flame or a flower and sit with it in silence as you concentrate on seeing every detail—the way the flame flickers, the different colors that appear, the shapes of the flower's petals, how they are attached to the stalk—as many details as you can discover that you wouldn't normally notice.

Anyone can use these exercises or "tricks" to help them harness the power of the mind and make it work for them.

out what you can do right now to change or improve your situation. There's always something, but you need to stop feeling sorry for yourself and blaming outside circumstances and start to take responsibility for turning things around. If you continue to believe that because you failed in the past you are destined to continue failing in the future, and that you might as well just give up and stop trying, you are making sure that your dire prediction is going to come true.

─── *A Word to the Wise* ───

To keep yourself thinking positively, remember to keep track of the small goals you achieve and give yourself the points you deserve for your effort.

Be Realistic

Anyone can dream the impossible dream, but when we open our eyes in the morning we need to get back to reality. I may dream all I want about waking up to discover that I've been transformed into George Clooney overnight, but the minute I look in the mirror that dream will be over. Remember that I've already said this isn't magic.

What this means is that, if your dearest wish or biggest dream is to become a corporate lawyer, you need to have a law degree, or go to law school, or remold that dream into something more realistic, like becoming a paralegal.

I'm not saying that you can't do or be anything you want so long as your goals are within your control. I can't turn myself into George Clooney or Michael Jordan, but that doesn't mean I can't lose weight or get more fit or play a game of pickup basketball.

So again, focus on what you want, send out positive thoughts, commit to the process, and do what it takes.

Don't Be Afraid to Follow Your Passion

Following your passion is probably the surest way of bringing more of what you want into your life. I truly believe that most people have some idea of what they're passionate about. Unfortunately, too many of us are afraid to take the chance and make the changes that would allow us to do what we love.

Cynthia was a born entrepreneur. She was extremely intelligent, had an MBA, and was full of energy—practically bursting with about sixteen ideas for different businesses she could start. The problem was that not one of her ideas ever got off the ground because she could never focus on doing just one thing at a time or even decide what that one thing ought to be. As we talked, Cynthia indicated that the one thing she was truly passionate about was animals. She loved animals and had even come up with an organic, all-natural recipe for dog biscuits that she baked at home for her own dogs. It seemed strange to me that not one of the business ideas she'd mentioned had anything to do with animals. I asked her why she hadn't thought of using her valuable marketing skills to turn her passion and her recipe into a business. What she told me was that she'd never considered using her intelligence and education for something that seemed to her so inconsequential. It was all well and good to make biscuits for her dogs, but was that really the basis for a business?

I assured her that turning her passion to profit was the best way I knew to make her both financially comfortable and content. Once she'd thought about that, she began to find her focus. Her original dog biscuit recipe has now expanded into a company that produces and markets a whole line of organic, eco-friendly pet products.

In another case, a client and her late husband had been passionate about encouraging and collecting the work of new artists. They both had a good eye, and they spent practically every weekend going to various galleries. Many of the young artists whose work they'd bought over the years turned out to be very successful, and the value of the works they had bought had increased exponentially. Nevertheless, they'd never thought of turning their passion into a profession. After her husband died, my client was at a loss. She missed her husband and she missed the pleasure they'd gotten from their hobby. As we talked, I suggested that she try to find a way to turn their mutual love of collecting into a business. When she thought about it, she realized that she didn't want to sell any of the paintings they'd bought together but that she could continue to buy new art, help emerging artists, and honor her husband's memory all at once by opening a gallery representing young artists. In the end, she did exactly that, and both she and her gallery are now thriving.

Just don't give up trying to do what you really want to do. Where there is love and inspiration, I don't think you can go wrong.

—Ella Fitzgerald

Why is it that so many of us think we can't or shouldn't make a living doing what we love? If you love something, chances are it's also something you've learned a lot about or it's an area in which you have a particular skill. Use your knowledge and your skill so that your love becomes your life's work. By doing that you will find fulfillment and your cornucopia of prosperity will be full to overflowing.

A Checklist for a Treasure Chest Full of Prosperity

✓ *Prioritize your goals and begin with what is most achievable so that you experience some success.*

✓ *Focus and be extremely specific. The more clearly you can visualize what you want, the more likely it is that you can bring it into your life.*

✓ *Commit to the Three C's: be constant, consistent, and creative.*

✓ *Be realistic. Think big but don't ask for the impossible.*

✓ *Create a mental motion picture of your prosperous future. Use all your senses to see yourself in the place you most want to be.*

✓ *Counteract each negative thought with two positives. Your mind is extremely powerful and will manifest whatever it is you think about most.*

✓ *Put some EFFORT into it. Use your positive energy; have faith that it will happen; focus on your goal; get organized; use your resolve, and be tenacious.*

✓ *Follow your passion; it's passion that will keep you going when times are tough.*

SEEK MORE SPIRITUAL STRENGTH

Many people link spirituality to participation in some form of organized religion. For some people spirituality may well be linked to traditional religious beliefs, but I believe that there is no one right or wrong way to seek or achieve spirituality.

Some time ago I received a call from a woman who had been to see me and who had subsequently been told by members of her church that what I did was "the work of the devil" and that by consulting me she had committed a sin. So I asked her what *she* thought, and she told me that when she looked into my eyes she'd realized I'd been given a gift from God and that there was no way she could *not* believe in me.

Then, more recently, a rabbi came to see me in my office, because, she told me, so many members of her congregation were telling her how

We are not human beings on a spiritual journey. We are spiritual beings on a human journey.

—Stephen Covey

much I had helped them. "You truly have a gift," she told me. "I don't understand it, but I see it as something that can make a difference in helping people. I deal with people's spiritual side, but you are able to mend fences I don't even see. I know they exist, but I don't know how to get there." I felt honored by what she said, but, as I told her, she too had a gift—the gift of open-mindedness and the ability to understand that each of us was trying to do the same thing, which was to bring people more spiritual peace.

I have always felt very strongly that it is not my role to impose my own particular spiritual beliefs on anyone else. In fact, I coach people all the time to remember that their own spiritual beliefs are personal and should be kept private. Very often I'm hired to do readings at corporate events. On these occasions it's very important that not only I but also the company that's hired me be sensitive to the possibility that not everyone will be open to what I do and that no one should feel coerced into participating unless they're comfortable doing so. Not so long ago, at one of these events, two people in the audience were trying to prevent their colleagues from approaching me and asking for readings. I politely let them know that while I respected their personal beliefs, they needed to be equally respectful of the choices their coworkers were making.

I would urge everyone to find his or her own road to increased spiritual strength. As you discover your spiritual self, you unwrap a gift of love for yourself, for those around you, and for what you have in your life that reaches farther than your mind and deeper than the core of your heart. Simply put, to be spiritual is to have faith and hope—faith that there is a higher power and that there is more to life than physical existence on this plane of being; hope that even when life is at its most difficult, whatever is happening happens for a reason and that things will get better. With that faith and hope, we become better able to deal with the disappointments and setbacks that are certain to appear in our lives.

Sometimes it can feel as if we're caught in a dangerous rip current and are about to drown. What we need to remember is that when we're caught in a rip current we need to swim with it and eventually we'll come out into safe waters and be able to swim ashore. Having faith is not much different from believing that if we commit ourselves to swimming with the current we will ultimately reach a safe haven.

Spirituality Resides Within

Many people seem to believe that they have to go to some far-off place like the mountains of Tibet or an ashram in India to find spirituality. But that isn't so. Spirituality is to be found wherever you are right now. If you're looking for it, you need to look inward, not outward. It's not going to be a perfect process. What you're trying to do is shed the bad habits and negative thoughts that are preventing your best self from shining through. You can think of your higher self as a sun hidden behind layers of clouds. Each time a layer dissipates, the sunshine becomes stronger.

The more you are able to increase your spirituality, the more you will come to understand that you are not becoming a different person; you are simply becoming a better version of yourself.

Spirituality in Good Times and Bad

When things are going well for us, it's easy to believe we're in charge of our own destiny and we're doing everything right. Then, when life hands us a blow, we tend to bring in the God factor, either blaming God for punishing us or praying to the higher power to save us—sometimes both at once. Either way, what this means is that we are once again abdicating responsibility for ourselves and the choices we make.

What many people don't understand is that there's an all-important difference between having faith in a higher power (or God, if that's what you wish to call it) and believing that whatever happens to us is the will of God. One leads to the understanding that our lives have greater meaning; the other leads to the misunderstanding that we have no power over our lives.

Yes, certainly we are tested and tried—some more than others. But, for the most part, we create those tests and trials for ourselves, because we have free will. I believe that we are all put on this earth to learn. We have control over our thoughts and our actions; we have control over how we react to our circumstances, and we can either learn from our experiences, which creates growth and change, or we can

THE BENEFITS OF SPIRITUALITY

A Sense of Security and Safety

When we experience connection with a higher power we feel less alone and adrift in the world. We become aware that there is a power greater than ourselves at work in the universe.

Inner Peace

Knowing that we are being guided by a higher power reduces stress and anxiety because we can rest assured, even when things are at their most difficult, that we are not merely victims of bad luck and that this situation was meant to be. Whatever is going on in the world outside you will no longer have the power to affect your moods and emotions.

Self-Awareness

The more we connect with our higher selves the more aware we become of our innate ability to become better. One important component of increased spirituality is a heightened awareness of our core values and what it means to be true to ourselves as we move through life.

The Ability to Give and Receive Unconditional Love

The more we are able to open ourselves to the experience of God or a higher power, the more we will experience what it feels like to be loved unconditionally and the better able we will be to show unconditional love to those around us.

stubbornly refuse to believe that we have the ability to create change for ourselves. God doesn't *make* us do anything. In fact, God doesn't care if we believe in Him or not; that's our issue, not His.

The point is to work on increasing our spiritual practice when times are good so that our connection to the higher power will be there to sustain us when times are bad. If we don't thank the higher power for our gifts, how can we then rage at God when things go wrong? You can't have it both ways.

Having hope and faith means believing that no matter how bad life may seem right now, it isn't going to stay that way. It will get better. Furthermore, whatever we're going through in the present is part of our path.

Two of my clients provide perfect examples of how differently people can respond to equally tragic experiences. Both are mothers; both lost their children to devastating illnesses when they were still in their teens; both had traditional religious affiliations.

One of these women, whose name was Margaret, became so angry at God when her son died after a long battle with stomach cancer that she temporarily lost her faith and couldn't allow herself to heal. When I met with her, she was still furious. How could God have done this to her? How could He have taken her wonderful, bright boy at such a young age? I gently reminded her that her son had suffered for four years and never complained. In fact, he had hung on to life until he felt that she was strong enough to survive his loss. All the time he was ill, he was thinking about her. He had both true faith and an unconditional love of life, and I could think of no more powerful expression of spirituality than that. He wasn't angry with God, so why should she be? I hoped that once she was able not only to mourn his death but also to appreciate his life, she would also be able to learn and take comfort from the way he had lived.

The other woman's son had been diagnosed with type 1 diabetes when he was a small child and ultimately went into a diabetic coma and died when he was just a teenager. In this instance the strength and grace with which he had faced and dealt with his illness throughout his short life so inspired his mother that after his death she felt called to enter the ministry.

What is the lesson to be learned from these two women? I believe it is this: If we look upon adversity as a punishment, that's what it will be. If we look upon adversity as an invitation to grow, it will make us stronger and wiser.

Mike, yet another of my clients, was the survivor of a horrendous car accident involving five vehicles, including a tractor-trailer, that resulted in four fatalities. Mike, who survived against all odds, had always been a carefree, party-loving guy who pretty much did whatever he pleased without giving much thought to how it might affect other people. Since the accident, however, he has turned into someone who is now exquisitely conscious of the fact that every one of our actions has a reaction and that we must therefore take responsibility for our own actions (even though he had in no way been responsible for the accident).

In my work I've found that very often people who've had a close brush with death come back from the experience with a greater understanding of their own paths and a need to find greater meaning in their lives—which is really just another way of saying that they are seeking more spirituality.

Find Spirituality in Adversity

When I met Elizabeth, I was amazed by the spiritual strength she'd managed to create for herself despite terrible personal tragedy. Her son and one of his college roommates had died in a dormitory fire that was inadvertently set by a third roommate, who was the only survivor. Elizabeth could have railed at fate; she could have taken out her anger against the survivor who had started the fire; she could even have brought charges against the school for having failed to put smoke alarms in the dorm rooms. But she didn't do any of that. When I asked how she had managed to find so much forgiveness in her heart, she told me that she knew her kind and caring son well enough to understand that he wouldn't have wanted her to be vindictive. Instead, she had dug deep within herself and chosen to honor his memory and his spirit by establishing a scholarship in his name at the college. There is probably no greater loss than the loss of a child, but Elizabeth was able to turn her son's death into something that enriched her spirit and ensured that his legacy would not be forgotten.

I've actually found that very often people are able to create something good and positive out of the most negative circumstances. I met one of those people at a luncheon to raise funds for breast cancer research. Gloria came up to me after the luncheon to thank me for the work I do on behalf of the Walk for Women Breast Cancer Fund and to tell me about her own campaign to raise funds and awareness for a very different kind of medical problem. She told me that one of her three children had been born with severe combined immunodeficiency disorder (SCID), which meant that the slightest infection could potentially prove fatal. Like Elizabeth, however, Gloria had found strength in her adversity and was doing everything in her power to help eradicate the disease.

Character cannot be developed in ease and quiet. Only through experience of trial and suffering can the soul be strengthened, ambition inspired, and success achieved.

—Helen Keller

Both of these women personify what I consider to be true spirituality—faith and hope combined with a deep-rooted inner strength.

Anger Is Always Self-Destructive

A gentleman came to me because his life was a mess. His wife had died of cancer, his brother had been murdered, and now his seventeen-year-old son had run away from home. My client, Milton, was a successful businessman, but his business was just about the only aspect of his life that was going well. He was furious about all the terrible things that had happened to him, and now his anger was carrying over into his relationships.

Although it was certainly true that he'd had to deal with some terrible tragedies, Milton was really making things worse for himself, because his anger and negativity were driving away the people who most cared about him and who would otherwise have been a source of support. What he needed to understand and accept was that he was allowing his past to dictate his life in the present. And by taking out his anger on everyone around him, he was actually ensuring that he would remain isolated and lonely, which would only make him angrier. In other words, he was setting up a vicious cycle that only he could end by letting go of his anger.

Whether it's directed at God, at other people, or at yourself, anger always prevents you from finding any kind of peace. This was certainly true of the self-blaming woman who asked for my help after her teenage son committed suicide. He'd been exhibiting symptoms of depression for some time—not sleeping, acting out, isolating himself in his room—and now she was angry with herself for not recognizing his mental state and forcing him into therapy. All she kept saying was, "I should have known. I should have done something about it." But, as I explained to her, there was no way she could have prevented him from taking his own life. That was his path, his decision, and she wasn't to blame for his action. Until she could believe that and stop being angry with herself, she would never be able to move on with her own life.

Character—the willingness to accept responsibility for one's own life—is the source from which self-respect springs.

—Joan Didion

Once we stop being angry with ourselves, we will be able to nurture ourselves. We need to do that if we are ever to achieve inner peace.

———— *A Word to the Wise* ————

In the end, we all seek serenity. When you're angry or
upset, you need to think about how to find peace.

I believe that one of the most powerful ways we have to release
our anger is to become more aware of our gifts. I make it a ritual, when
I get up each morning, to thank the higher power for what I've been
given—a beautiful wife, two beautiful children, a roof over my head,
the ability to help other people. As we become conscious of all our
gifts, it becomes more and more difficult to stay angry. The more gratitude you feel, the more inner peace you will have.

We Are All Responsible

All of us are responsible for our own actions, but some people prefer
to think of having faith in a higher power as a way to abdicate responsibility, an excuse just to sit back and wait to see what's going to happen
to them. And then, if they don't like the way things are going, they can
blame God for having done it to them. Or, if they do something wrong,
they prefer to believe that the devil made them do it. But that's not
what spirituality is about at all.

If you pray to God to give you something, and what you receive is
not exactly what you asked for, you might decide there is no God after

all or that God is punishing you. If you pray instead for guidance or help in solving a problem, you are acknowledging the higher power while at the same time accepting responsibility for yourself. Asking for that kind of guidance is exactly what lies at the heart of all twelve-step self-help programs.

True spirituality is about the search for meaning; it's about discovering our true paths, the meaning and purpose of our lives. We're all here for a reason. We're here to learn; it just takes some of us longer than others to figure out what we're supposed to be learning.

Learn to Recognize the Right Path when You're on It

Ruthie was a client who failed to recognize her purpose even though it was right in front of her every day. When she told me that she wasn't sure her life really had value, all I could do was stare at her in amazement. Over many years, Ruthie and her husband have been foster parents to more than thirty children—and still counting. Some of the children she and her husband have adopted, others have stayed with them only temporarily, but she's made such a great impact on all of them that she has, in many instances, literally saved their lives. Although Ruthie and her husband never had a lot of money, they have an abundance of love and a compelling need to help. Some of the older children, who are now grown up, have gone on to marry and have children of their own, so they are passing on the values she instilled in them to the next generation. In other words, what Ruthie has done with her life will make a difference long after she herself is gone.

What she was doing, however, came so naturally to her that she honestly didn't see it as being important enough to be meaningful. The point I had to make to her is that a life of value isn't necessarily lived on the public or world stage. We don't have to invent the internal combustion engine or eradicate world hunger in order for our lives to have meaning. If we live with compassion, generosity, and commitment, if we give back as much or more than we receive, we are living a spiritual life—a life that enriches the souls of others as well as our own. In fact, the lives of those who do not receive recognition often have a greater impact on those they touch than the lives of those who are publicly rewarded.

Spirituality Is Something We're Born with and Need to Nurture

Yes, that's correct. We all come into this world with the knowledge that there is a higher plane, a soul world, which is where we come from and where we will return. The problem is that the more involved we get with the nitty-gritty of everyday life, the more likely we are to lose that innate connection to our higher selves.

People come into my office all the time telling me that they want to become spiritual, and I have to explain to them that we don't "become" spiritual. Spirituality isn't something we acquire; it's something already within us that we have to seek out, nurture, and fine-tune throughout our lives. That takes work; it takes commitment.

Spirituality is like a seed that, as I've said, is born within us and that we need to feed and nurture. Our soul is a living organism that requires nourishment just as our bodies require food to grow and thrive. That means taking the time to tune out all the noise and the distractions that are coming at us all the time, every day, and quieting our minds.

And then, when we go back out into the world, we need to take our spiritual selves with us. It isn't enough to go into a room and meditate or pray. We then have to *act out* what we've brought into our lives in the way we go about our business on a daily basis. We need to live our lives with honesty, humility, and heart. Be more tolerant and considerate. Develop the habit of committing at least one small act of kindness every day. Help an elderly person across the street or remember to say thank you for a service. These little things make a big difference, and if we do them every day, we will be turning our everyday environment into a sacred place.

— A Word to the Wise —

The Latin word *anima* means "soul" or "breath of life." When you seek spirituality, you're looking for the breath that feeds your soul.

I believe that meditation is extremely important for our spiritual well-being; I believe that prayer is important for connecting with the higher power. When people tell me they don't have time for meditation and prayer, I ask them, Do you want to do the work or do you just want to talk about it? How about saying a few prayers instead of listening to the radio while you're on your way to work? How about taking a few minutes to meditate instead of turning on the television as soon as you get home in the evening? Once you're willing to put out that energy, you'll be amazed at what you get back.

In the Bible, God himself exhorts us to meditate. In the book of Joshua 1:8–9 the Lord speaks to Joshua and tells him

> this book of the law shall not depart out of thy mouth; but thou shalt meditate therein day and night, that thou mayest observe to do according to all that is written therein: for then thou shalt make thy way prosperous, and then thou shalt have good success.
>
> Have I not commanded thee? Be strong and of good courage; be not afraid, neither be thou dismayed: for the LORD thy God is with thee whithersoever thou goest.

Although meditation has come to be associated with Eastern and New Age religious practices, the word "meditate" appears fourteen times and the word "meditation" six times in the King James Version of the Bible.

That said, it's worth repeating here that being spiritual doesn't require you to belong to an organized religious community. It doesn't require you to go to a church or a temple or a mosque to connect with your higher power—although that may be the path some people choose to take. At the same time, neither should meditation or seeking any other way to connect with your higher self or a higher power conflict with any other belief system to which you might adhere.

———— *A Word to the Wise* ————

You have to do the prep work to develop
your spirituality—the same way an athlete
or a musician needs to practice. That's
why it's called "spiritual practice."

Many people have asked me to teach them how to pray, but that isn't really possible. Every religion and every culture has adopted specific prayers offered to particular deities and for particular occasions. Finding the prayer or prayers that facilitate your own connection with a higher power is perhaps the most personal decision you can make. If you belong to a particular religion, look in the prayer book of your faith; if you are interested in discovering how other people voice their prayers, consult their prayer books or even search for prayers on the Internet. If you want something that is unique and uniquely meaningful to you, make it up. Just don't think that what anyone else does to create a connection is necessarily what will work for you—it might be, but then again it might not.

Create Your Own Rituals

People seem to think that there is a right way and a wrong way to confirm their hope and faith or to gain clarity about their life's purpose, but there isn't. All you have to do is commit to finding the way of connecting that works for you.

If you're comfortable in a traditional house of worship, by all means go there. But if you feel closest to the higher power sitting on the beach, in the woods, or by the side of a lake, make that place your own house of worship. The higher power will be there to meet you wherever you seek it.

As I've said, I take things from many cultures and belief systems. I've already described my own morning meditation ritual (pages 113 and 114). Also, on the desk in my office I have a statue of the Buddha as well as a number of Native American religious artifacts and the Tibetan bell I've already told you about. Alongside those articles I also have representations of St. Anthony and St. Jude. St. Anthony is the patron saint of lost and stolen articles and St. Jude is the patron saint of lost causes and people in need. Because of the work I do helping people to heal after losing a loved one or losing their way, I find that these particular saints keep me mindful of the responsibilities that come with my gift.

In addition, spending so much time dealing with the negativity of others, I could easily fall into negative patterns of thought and lose touch with my own faith and hope. Having these objects around me every day reminds me of my commitment not only to helping my clients but also to nurturing my own spiritual self.

I should point out, however, that I have chosen these objects and artifacts because each one has a particular meaning for *me*. What I think people need to be careful of is going on what I like to call a spiritual wild goose chase. When you start down a spiritual path, it can be tempting to align yourself with someone else's spiritual identity simply because you want to belong somewhere. However, the point is not to adjust yourself to the belief system of another person or of a group but to seek your own spiritual identity by getting in touch with the core of who *you* really are.

> *Today you are You, that is truer than true. There's no one alive who is Youer than You.*
>
> **—Dr. Seuss**

The More You Put Out, the More You Receive

Commitment is a big part of spirituality. There's no shortcut to becoming a more spiritual person. It's just like anything else you want to bring into your life: the more energy you commit to it the more you'll get

WRITE YOUR OWN MANUAL
FOR HOW TO LIVE YOUR LIFE

'm a strong believer in the power of spontaneous journaling.

When you get up in the morning, while you're having your first cup of coffee or tea, take a few minutes to write down what you want to bring into your life and what you want to work on that day. Then, whenever you have a quiet moment, go back to what you've written and consider where those thoughts came from. How does what you wrote relate to your long- and short-term goals for yourself? How does it relate to what you fear or what you hope for? How does it relate to what you want to bring into your life? Once you listen to your inner voice and write down what it's telling you, you will become better able to believe it. From there you can begin to ask yourself what you need to do to reach the goals you aspire to and become the person you truly want to be.

Random thoughts are fleeting, but if you can capture them on paper for later consideration, you can learn a lot about your inner life that might otherwise be lost in the turmoil of external experience.

back. If you put little or nothing into it, you'll receive little or nothing in return.

—— *A Word to the Wise* ——

Think of your life as a big pot of chicken soup bubbling away on the stove. The more good ingredients you add to the pot, the richer and more nourishing your soup will become.

People who are caught up in a negative, "woe is me" frame of mind tell me all the time that they don't have a guardian angel. But they do. We all do. They're simply not willing to commit to making the connection. As I tell them, the more positive energy you put out the more you'll get back and, therefore, the more you'll believe. You can even ask for a sign and you'll receive one. It may not be what you expected, and it probably won't be accompanied by blaring trumpets and thunder from the heavens, but if you're alert, you will recognize it.

One of the most powerful signs I've ever heard about came to one of my clients after she prayed for a sign from her deceased mother. That night, she had a dream in which her parents were sitting in the pair of Barcaloungers she had in her living room. When she got up the next morning her husband asked her if she'd been up during the night. She told him she hadn't and asked him why. "Because," he said, "when I went into the living room this morning the lounge chairs were in the reclining position and I know I put them upright before I went to bed last night." My client, of course, broke down in tears because she knew her prayer had been answered.

In another instance a woman had asked for a sign from her mother, whose favorite color had been blue. The woman was in the supermarket in the aisle with the fresh flowers when she looked up and saw bunches of blue roses. She'd never seen blue roses before and asked the clerk if the store always carried them. "No," he said. "It must have been a mistake because we've never had them before."

And finally there is the woman who regularly attends every event I have in the area where she lives. Her son died in a boating accident, and she'd had a very difficult time coming to terms with the way he died. Once I was able to assure her that he was at peace, she too found peace within herself, and since then, she tells me, she receives signs from him on a regular basis.

Learn to get in touch with the silence within yourself, and know that everything in life has purpose. There are no mistakes, no coincidences, all events are blessings given to us to learn from.

—Elisabeth Kübler-Ross

A Word to the Wise

The first step toward spiritual growth is to keep an open mind. If you close yourself off, you won't be receptive to receiving what is possible.

Maybe your mother always wore Shalimar perfume and while you're alone in your home you suddenly smell her scent. Or maybe you have fond childhood memories of your dad smoking his pipe after dinner and when you're thinking about something entirely different you become aware of the smell of his tobacco. Those are signs. You're not making them up; rather, you're opening yourself up to the possibility of an eternal life beyond your life on *terra firma*.

Seek and You Shall Find

Throughout history and the history of the world's religions, there have been seekers who left their communities and everyday lives to find a higher self and connect with a higher purpose. Dante's *Divine Comedy*, perhaps the greatest allegory of all time, describes man's search for higher meaning within the context of Christianity. But we find seekers in the Old and New Testaments of the Bible and across the world's religions.

In Exodus Moses goes up to Mt. Sinai and receives the word of God, which he then brings back to his people. In Mark, Jesus goes into the wilderness for forty days and forty nights to fast, pray, and prepare for his ministry.

And in the Buddhist tradition we have the story of Siddhartha Gautama, who leaves his wealthy family to begin a six-year quest for enlightenment, after which he returns to the world to teach what he has learned.

In modern literature, books as diverse as *Cold Mountain* and *Zen and the Art of Motorcycle Maintenance* that revolve around a journey that results in spiritual growth continue to capture our attention.

Whether or not you regard any of these stories as historical fact within the context of your own belief system, what they tell us about

BE AWARE OF SYNCHRONICITIES
IN YOUR LIFE

The great Swiss psychoanalyst Carl Jung coined the term "synchronicity" to define what he called meaningful coincidences in your life. For example, if you were just thinking about a particular person you hadn't spoken to in a long time and that person happened to call just at the moment you were thinking of him, that would be a synchronicity.

I believe that these synchronicities are the higher power's way of letting you know that you are on the right path. If you find these events occurring and you don't understand why, it's time to start paying attention and opening yourself up to seeing where they lead you.

man's quest for higher meaning clearly resonates, one way or another, with our own search for a deeper spirituality in our lives.

Beyond that, however, what is significant about each of these stories is that at the end of his quest, the seeker returns to share what he's learned. Spirituality isn't just about looking within ourselves; it's also about living in the here and now, bringing what we've learned into the context of our everyday lives and sharing it with those around us.

The Gift That Keeps on Giving

Spirituality is the paradigmatic gift that keeps on giving. It is one of the greatest treasures you can bring into your life because it is what will get you through the dark days and the hard times that you will surely encounter as you continue on the path of your life. As you start on the road toward developing your own spirituality, you need to believe that you will arrive at a place of comfort.

A Word to the Wise

Joy and sorrow go together. We couldn't appreciate one if we didn't also experience the other.

If you continue to cultivate and strengthen your link with your higher self and the higher power by devoting yourself to whatever spiritual practices you choose to follow on a regular basis, you will find that your entire life becomes richer and fuller and that you appreciate what you have rather than being angry, frustrated, and disappointed because of what you don't have.

FIND YOUR OWN COMFORT ZONE

If your environment is cluttered or disorganized or simply uncomfortable, it will impede the flow of mental energy that allows you to connect to your higher self and the higher power. Think about where you feel most comfortable and at peace. For some people it might be a quiet beach, for another a cozy seat by a roaring fire. Some people even find peace riding alone in a car on the wide-open road. Wherever you find your own comfort zone, try to get there as often as possible to forget your daily distractions and open your mind to a greater truth.

A Checklist for Filling Your Spiritual Treasure Chest

✓ *Understand that spirituality doesn't require you to follow any organized religion unless you choose to.*

✓ *Understand that, if you do adhere to any particular religion, seeking more spirituality will enhance your religious experience.*

✓ *Become a seeker by embarking on a personal quest for spiritual growth. Enhancing spiritual strength takes commitment and consistency.*

✓ *Find the time to quiet your mind and engage with your inner self through meditation on a regular basis. There is no right or wrong way to meditate.*

✓ *Keep a spiritual journal to create a manual for how you live your life.*

✓ *Find a prayer or prayers that facilitate your connection with the higher power.*

✓ *Bring your spiritual experiences into your everyday life. Your behavior needs to match your spiritual growth.*

✓ *Don't fall into the "woe is me" fallacy and blame God or the higher power for your problems. Instead, look upon those problems as opportunities to learn and grow.*

✓ *Look to your spiritual self for the strength to get through life's difficulties and disappointments.*

✓ *Remember to nurture your faith and your hope.*

MAINTAIN YOUR EMOTIONAL AND PHYSICAL HEALTH— SOME PRACTICAL TIPS

We all know that we have to give equal attention to nurturing body, mind, and spirit. Physical aches and pains can be manifestations of spiritual or emotional pain; conversely, alleviating your physical pain can have a reciprocal effect on you emotional health. To take care of yourself emotionally you need to be consistent about living your life in accordance with what I call "the Three B's."

Man's troubles are rooted in extreme attention to senses, thoughts, and imagination. Attention should be focused internally to experience a quiet body and a calm mind.

—Buddha

1. *Be grateful (for what you have).*

The more you focus on what you do have rather than on what you don't, the more positive energy you'll be putting out into the world and the more positive energy you will attract. We're all good at coming up with lists of all the bad things in our lives. Instead, sit down and make a list of the top ten things in your life for which you are grateful.

2. *Be forgiving.*

People in general find it hard to forgive, but being angry all the time not only puts you in a bad place emotionally, it also puts stress on your body. Holding on to anger is self-defeating; letting it go sets you free.

3. *Be at peace with yourself (and trust your process).*

When you're at peace with the path of your own life it's much easier to make peace with the people around you. If you're always fighting with yourself, that attitude will carry over into all your relationships. Until you can make peace with your past and your present, you won't be able to change your future.

──────── A Word to the Wise ────────

Inner peace comes from inside you, not from outward circumstances—that's why it's called "inner" peace.

FOUR STRATEGIES FOR DIFFUSING ANGER AND REDUCING STRESS

1. *Don't take it personally.*

People are carrying around their own anger and resentments, and what you need to remember is that when they let it out, it's not about you. It's about them. Furthermore, when bad things happen—as they will—they are not directed at you personally. The driver did not speed through the puddle in order to splash you; you just happened to be standing in the way of the splash.

2. *Don't respond.*

If someone is venting his or her anger at you, take a step back, remind yourself that it's not about you, and don't continue the argument. The temptation is always to defend ourselves, but that's only going to prolong the angry conversation. You probably won't win and you'll only be taking on anger that wasn't yours to begin with.

3. *Learn to be more tolerant.*

Try not to sweat the small stuff. If you let every little irritant get to you, you'll be carrying more stress than you need to. I like to tell people that they need to stop acting like a bellhop and put down all that baggage they're carrying around.

4. *Learn that you can't fix every problem.*

You're not Atlas and you can't carry the weight of the world on your shoulders. If someone else is having a problem, remind yourself that it's her problem and you're not required to take on her burden.

Soothe Yourself with a Healing Bath

When you feel negativity building up, wash it away—literally. Fill your bath and add sea salts, lavender oil, lemon oil, or whatever you find soothing. Then, as you wash each part of your body, tell yourself that you are releasing all the negative thoughts and emotions you've allowed to build up inside you. Just as I suggest that you clear any lingering stagnant or negative energy from your living or work space, you can do the same thing for your body.

When you get dressed, imagine yourself putting on a pure white coat that is going to protect you from dark thoughts and toxic emotions. You can do this several times a week, or as often as you feel necessary to keep yourself in a positive frame of mind.

A Word to the Wise

When you don't like the place you're in, do a
visualization and put yourself in a better place—
like a beach on an island in the Caribbean.

THREE SIMPLE STEPS
TO NEGATE NEGATIVITY

1. Become more aware of when negative thoughts start to percolate in your mind, and just tell yourself, "Stop it." You can do that. We can all choose where we focus our mental and emotional energy.

2. Now, think of all the times you've experienced peace, love, joy, compassion, good health. Become conscious of those moments and frame them. We all know how to cling to worries; instead, learn to cling to joys.

3. Be proactive. Make something good happen instead of waiting for it to come to you.

Learn to Love the Sound of Silence

People come to me every day because they want to know if they're on the right path, because they feel they're in a rut, or because they need validation for what their gut is telling them to do. Basically, they're unhappy, and they want me to use my insight to help them change. Very often I am able to do that, but I also believe that we all have an inner voice that's telling us how to be happy. The problem is that very often it speaks so quietly that we are able to ignore it. To hear it, you need to sit still, be quiet, and listen.

EIGHT EASY WAYS TO LIVE
A BETTER LIFE TODAY

1. Get up on the right side of the bed and tell yourself you're going to have a good day.

2. Remind yourself of all the people who love and appreciate you, and let them know how much you appreciate them.

3. Reward yourself for the good things you do in order to keep yourself motivated.

4. Give a gift to someone you love.

5. Give someone a hug.

6. Perform a little act of kindness every day.

7. Take a risk; change can be scary, but there is no change without change.

8. Slow down the process. Don't make hasty decisions. Step back, take a deep breath, and be patient. Not everything you want is going to happen right away.

Most of us have a hard time with silence. We'd rather distract ourselves with noise—from the television, an iPod, or just the distractions of daily events—than silence it so that we can hear what our inner voice is trying to tell us. I believe we get hunches all the time; we're just afraid to acknowledge or follow them.

—————— *A Word to the Wise* ——————

If you can manage your mind, you can manage your stress.

Many years ago a gentleman came to see me because he wasn't satisfied with his career even though he was running a successful catering business. It turned out that what he really enjoyed about catering parties was the voyeuristic pleasure of getting to see the inside of other people's homes. When he told me that, I suggested he take a course in how to appraise properties. That way he could satisfy his curiosity about the way people lived without having to cook his way into their house. He actually thought that was a great idea; twenty years later he came back and told me how happy he was and that I had changed his life.

Then there were two young women I remember very clearly who were in the television news business. One was a weather person in New York who was moving across the country and concerned about how much her life was going to change. We discussed the pros and cons and I assured her that she'd find new opportunities on the West Coast and that ultimately she'd be much happier. She made the move and, not long after, she met a man, settled down, and is now very happy with her new life. But she needed my reassurance before she was able to take the plunge. The other was a reporter who had been offered two jobs and didn't know whether to accept the one in California or the one in Texas. My prediction was that if she chose to go to Texas she'd be walking into a crisis situation and would have a real opportunity to make her mark. Sure enough, she went, and less than two weeks later Hurricane Ike crashed ashore and she was working round the clock.

I have no doubt that these people—and the many others who have come to me to get some direction about what they should be doing with their lives—truly believe that I changed their lives. But, in fact, I didn't. I can provide my insights, but changing one's life is always up to the person whose life it is.

Very often my clients come because they somehow want me to take responsibility for the choices they make. It's particularly disturbing to me that so many people want me to tell them whether or not they should end a marriage or a relationship. I can help them to gain more insight and, I hope, to see things more clearly. I can even reinforce decisions they've really come to on their own. But in the end we are all responsible for our own lives and our own relationships. I can make suggestions; I can try to help them; but I can't make decisions for them and I can't *make* them do anything. Most important, however, these people, and you too, can do what I do if you will only learn how to sit quietly with yourself, listen, trust your inner voice—and then act on what it's telling you.

As I tell my clients, the sound of silence is a beautiful thing.

—————— *A Word to the Wise* ——————

Take the time to find a quiet place and appreciate
the world around you—the beach, the country,
the birds, a sunset, a star-filled sky. You'll find
that becoming aware of the silence also quiets
the mind and brings emotional peace.

COLLEGE STUDENTS STUDY
HOW TO BE HAPPY

Early in 2009 an article in *Psychology Today* reported that the most popular class at Harvard University is about positive psychology and that at least one hundred other universities offer similar courses. The article then goes on to define happiness is and concludes that "neuroscientists, psychiatrists, behavioral economists, positive psychologists, and Buddhist monks" agree that it encompasses living a meaningful life, utilizing your gifts and your time, living with thought and purpose." And finally it states that people can "learn to internally challenge their negative assumptions . . . if not eliminate them altogether."

Naturally I was struck by how close that definition of happiness came to my own idea of finding your true path and living your life accordingly, and how similar the notion of challenging one's negative assumptions is to my advice that you take control of where you direct your emotional energy. It seems that I've been teaching positive psychology all along.

What Happens in Your Mind Affects What's Going on in Your Body

It stands to reason that a healthy mental attitude will make it easier to cope with whatever physical problems you might have. If you have the choice of whether to laugh or cry, it's generally better to laugh. We know that seeing the humor in an otherwise stressful situation can diffuse the tension and lighten the mood of the moment. I use this technique often when I'm doing a reading for a client who is making contact with the spirit of a loved one.

Beyond that, however, the science of gelotology (from the Greek *gelos*, "to laugh"), which is the study of humor and laughter and how it affects the human body, has found that having a good laugh can actually be beneficial to your health.

I'm sure you've heard the old adage "Laughter is the best medicine," but now we have scientific studies to prove that it's true. Among its many health benefits, several studies have shown that laughter can reduce levels of the stress hormone cortisol in the bloodstream, increase levels of endorphins (the hormones that are responsible for the runner's high), and bring more oxygen into the body—and, therefore, the brain.

The most wasted of all days is one without laughter.

—e. e. cummings

Fear, anxiety, and worry, on the other hand, manifest in the body as heart palpitations, light-headedness, a tightening of the stomach, and a tensing of the muscles that leads to neck or back pain.

What this means is that, quite simply, whatever we can do to maintain a positive emotional outlook will also have a positive effect on our physical health.

YOGA: THE UNION OF BODY AND MIND

The word "yoga" derives from the Sanskrit *yuj*, which means "to join or unite."

Although we in the West tend to emphasize the exercise component, the practice of yoga is intended as a way to integrate the body and the mind. The various poses are designed to revitalize the body by bringing fresh blood to the brain. The ultimate effect is to relax the body while calming the mind.

Because the movements are slow and fluid, yoga, unlike many other forms of physical exercise, allows the mind to slow down and, like meditation, encourages a sense of inner peace by asking practitioners to focus and look inward.

There are many styles of yoga, the most basic of which is hatha yoga. Ashtanga yoga is probably the most physically demanding because it is based on the constant flow of movement from one pose to another. Both vinyasa and kundalini yoga focus particularly on synchronizing breathing with the various poses. Kundalini yoga, in particular, is a meditative discipline that seeks to create communication between the mind and the body in order to promote psycho-spiritual growth.

—— *A Word to the Wise* ——

Releasing negative thoughts is a body-building experience.

Finding Renewal through Restful Sleep

We live in a world where we literally have to carve out the time to take care of ourselves both emotionally and physically. In a society that never sleeps because there is always business being transacted somewhere, we need to be consciously aware of allowing ourselves time to renew our physical and emotional energy. If we don't do that, we run the risk of losing ourselves along the way.

Corny as it may sound, one of the most important things we can do for ourselves is simply to sleep. That's one of the reasons I believe it's so important to get rid of your anger, resentments, jealousies, and other negative feelings that could otherwise disturb your sleep. Sleep is the ultimate shut-off valve. It quiets the conscious mind so that the unconscious can do its work. Why is it that the problems we thought were so serious the night before often seem a lot less troubling in the morning? Our subconscious has a way of putting things back into perspective, and that proverbial good night's sleep refuels the positive energy we need to find solutions.

To help yourself enhance your sleep, go back to key #3 and make sure that your bed and bedroom are providing a restful, restorative atmosphere. Remember that relaxation involves all your senses, so you'll want to be mindful of colors, textures, aromas, and sounds. You might want to light a scented candle and play soothing music or a meditation tape to take your mind off the difficulties you may have dealt with during the day. I like to remind people that bears hibernate in caves because the cave provides them with a sense of safety. Your bedroom should become your personal cave, the place of safety where you can release anxiety and rest in peace.

FIVE KEYS TO POSITIVE TIME MANAGEMENT

1. Take time to appreciate your loved ones.

2. Take time to appreciate yourself.

3. Take time to nurture your physical well-being.

4. Take time to see the beauty of the world around you.

5. Take time to embrace the moment.

Finding Balance in an Unbalanced World

Ellen came to see me because she was traumatized by guilt. She believed that she had somehow caused or at least contributed to the death of a coworker. It seems that Ellen had to leave the office early one evening and asked a colleague to cover for her. The next morning the colleague's body was found at her desk, where she'd died of a heart attack.

Ellen felt terrible about having asked the other woman to stay in her place and about not having thanked her properly. She was sure that if she hadn't asked her to stay, her colleague would still be alive. I understood that the situation must have been very upsetting, but it seemed to me that Ellen's reaction was unusually extreme. When I told her this, Ellen explained that her father had died riding the subway on his way to work one morning and that her colleague's death had brought up all the pain of that earlier experience. Even worse, she was feeling not only guilty but also frightened that she was on the same path—working herself literally to death.

This was a wake-up call she couldn't ignore, and it caused her to rethink her priorities. She vowed that from then on she would make it a point to create more time to take care of herself and be with her children. Eventually she even rearranged her schedule so that she was able to work from home two days a week.

Many times when mothers come to see me they're worried that their having to work is going to negatively impact their children. People are constantly being torn between the need to work longer hours and their fear of neglecting their families. I understand their concern because I too fight that battle every day. The hours that I work make it impossible for me to get home for dinner many nights, and as our children get older and have their own schedules, it becomes more and more difficult to plan those family meals. But we do the best we can. We make it a point to have at least three dinners together every week, and when we sit down together we make certain that we're all really *there*, talking and interacting with one another and not thinking about what we have to do next or what we didn't get done.

Creating balance is really a matter of determining what's important, getting organized, and making sure that we don't neglect one aspect of our life for another. If you're feeling guilty about spending time with your family when you could be working, or working when you could be spending time with your family, if you can't turn off your mind (or your BlackBerry) long enough to find some quiet time to restore your emotional equilibrium, if you neglect any aspect of yourself because you don't have the time to take care of yourself, you need to get back in balance.

Part of that process is to be sure you're not taking on guilt for things that you're not guilty of. We can't be responsible for everyone and everything every minute of every day. We have to do the best we can and then let go of the rest.

───────── *A Word to the Wise* ─────────

"No" is not a four-letter word. Take the time to nurture yourself instead of trying to please everyone else.

JUDY MARTIN TALKS ABOUT BALANCING YOUR WORK/LIFE EXPERIENCE

We're living in an always-on world. The search for work/life balance has become more of a debate than a reality in our 24/7 world.

Judy Martin is an Emmy award–winning broadcast journalist whose experiences following the 9/11 attacks led her to create what she calls the WorkLife Nation. For her, the question became, How can we navigate sensory overload, work with meaning and purpose, and cultivate resilience? She tackles those questions at her website, WorkLifeNation.com, where she interviews experts and shares stories of innovation on the cutting edge of work/life integration, as well as in her Practical Chaos lecture series and her meditation CD, *Practical Chaos: Reflections on Resilience.*

Here are some of the tips for dealing with moments of emotional turmoil and finding that balance that she has been kind enough to share with me and my readers.

1. Take a breath in a moment of chaos.

2. Hesitate from a place of wisdom before speaking from a place of fear and pain.

3. Give yourself permission to change your perception of the crisis.

4. Take the appropriate action to consume or conquer the chaos of the moment. In my case during 9/11 those actions were service and meditation.

The great WorkLife Merge is happening whether we like it or not. How we handle it is a matter of choice—from a place of fear or one of proactive personal responsibility. Here are seven concise tips offering an alternative to burnout so that you can not only survive but also thrive in our challenging environment.

1. *Give yourself permission to take a break.* We are all our own worst critics at home and at work. Give yourself permission to wind down, even for a few minutes a day, with a walk, exercise, a good book, or a movie.

2. *Explore your own brand of creativity.* If you like to write, speak, or have another artistic bent, think of ways to incorporate those skills in the workplace or in your family life.

3. *Journal on a consistent basis.* In times of frustration, saying what you want, when you want, regardless of the consequences, may create conflict at home and in the workplace, but venting your soul for your eyes only might give you a new perspective.

4. *Take joy in accomplishing small tasks.* Even if it's just the laundry or making a phone call, set a few goals for yourself each day. This can be an enormous help to alleviate anxiety. Procrastination makes it difficult to move forward.

5. *Embrace a personal identity independent of your business image.* When we become too identified with our job or a position of power, anything that challenges that identity may cause anxiety. Put more effort into activities outside of work; explore volunteering outside of the sector in

which you work; spend more time cultivating relationships; and expand your skill base into other sectors.

6. ***Design your own program to cultivate resilience.*** Think about what brings you to a place of calm and take time out of your day to slow the wheels of the mind. Whether it's meditating, playing tennis, or reading, out of silence comes creativity and vitality. That small break just might be the catalyst for a great idea.

7. ***Remember to breathe.*** The interaction of activity and paying attention to how you breathe requires concentration and will keep your mind focused on what is in front of you. Breathing is the healing elixir of life and is the greatest tool to calm the mind and body.

When we go to work we carry the sensory overload from family life, the morning news, and our aggravating commute. Add to that the demands of having to be productive in a competitive marketplace and it is easy to understand why some form of workplace meditation is crucial.

Seven Ways to Meditate at Work

1. Once you are seated comfortably wherever you choose to meditate, follow your breath in and out, a technique known as mindful breathing or pranayama. Notice the air going into your nostrils and out of your mouth. Your stomach should rise as you inhale; draw your navel in as you exhale.

2. If your mind wanders, try choosing an affirmation to repeat for a period of time. It can be a simple phrase or mantra. Take a long, deep breath and on the out breath repeat the word or phrase. Repeat for a few minutes.

3. If you can close your eyes for a few minutes, meditate on the sounds in your office or outside. Be a witness without judging what you hear.

4. Bring a book of short prayers or meditations to work. Read one passage every day. Meditate on that passage and how it relates to your work.

5. Purchase or download screen savers that are designed to induce meditation. A few times a day, focus on the visual for several minutes while keeping your breath steady. Also, check out websites that offer short visual and audio meditations. Often you can download them onto an iPod.

6. A big favorite: artistic desk toys. A mini Zen sandbox or garden can boost creativity while calming your mind. Try doodling with crayons, or purchase one of the meditation kits sold at many bookstores that include such items as a flameless candle, chimes, and chanting tapes.

7. Do a stream-of-consciousness exercise. Call up a blank screen and write whatever comes into your mind. Just get it out. You can then delete the entire page.

When you are at work it's not likely that you'll be able to sit in a full lotus (legs crossed) at your desk or have incense burning while playing a guided meditation on your iPod. Those who work from home have that luxury, but for the rest of us the question is, How can we meditate at work? I would argue the better question is, How can we not?

A Three-Minute Desk Meditation

1. Set your cell phone alarm for three minutes and close your eyes gently.

2. Sit comfortably, with your back upright against your chair. Most would advise that your feet should be planted on the floor, not crossed—but you need to do what is comfortable for you. Rest your hands lightly on your knees with palms facing up.

3. Gently close your eyes and breathe deeply, inhaling through your nose, deep into your lungs, for a count of three. Hold the breath for three counts, then release through your mouth exhaling to a count of three, then hold the breath for three more counts.

4. Continue the exercise, inhaling for three, holding for three, exhaling for three, and holding the out breath for three seconds.

5. When the alarm goes off, hold the space and take in three deep breaths through your nose and out through your mouth. Open your eyes.

A Word to the Wise

Take an "attitude break." Give yourself a few moments to engage your mind in a positive thought process. Think about something that gives you pleasure. When you do that, you'll actually feel your body relax along with your mind.

LEARN TO BREATHE

One of the most effective ways to enhance your physical and emotional health is just learning how to breathe properly.

When we're stressed out and rushing around all day, our breathing tends to become quick and shallow. We're not really getting all the oxygen we need into our lungs and, especially, into the brain.

What we need to do is take a few minutes every day to practice deep breathing exercises.

1. Sit comfortably with one hand on your abdomen and the other on your chest. When you take a deep breath, the hand on your abdomen should rise more than the one on your chest.

2. Exhale through your mouth and then take in a slow, deep breath through your nose. Imagine that you're trying to suck all the air there is out of the room.

3. Again exhale through your mouth slowly, to the count of eight.

4. Repeat four more times.

Each time you breathe in, think "relax." As you exhale, think "stress and tension." By doing this you'll be mentally reinforcing the purpose of the exercise, which is to reduce tension and increase relaxation.

If you take a few moments to do this exercise whenever you feel yourself becoming tense in the course of the day, you will actually feel your body begin to relax.

A Checklist for Gathering Physical and Emotional Treasures

✓ *Remember the Three B's: be grateful, be forgiving, be at peace with yourself.*

✓ *Be aware of a negative emotion; just tell yourself to stop it.*

✓ *Take time to recognize the beauty all around you and think of it as a gift.*

✓ *Learn to laugh—it heals the body as well as the mind.*

✓ *Learn to breathe.*

✓ *Take an attitude break.*

✓ *Remember to take the time to tune in, turn off, and drop out.*

✓ *Learn to love the sound of silence.*

CONSIDER AND CONSOLIDATE YOUR RICHES

Now that you've used all the keys at your disposal to unlock your life's treasures so that they can work for you, it's time to take stock of the riches you've accumulated and make sure they continue to support your intentions.

Look at the self-evaluation you completed in the chapter on key #1. What can you now add to your list of things that make you happy? Look at the list of things you said you wanted to improve and see how many you can now transfer to your "happy" list. Write them down so that you can literally see how far you've come.

Ordinary riches can be stolen, real riches cannot. In your soul are infinitely precious things that cannot be taken from you.

—Oscar Wilde

Based on the work you've done with the help of this book, there are goals you may actually want to add or change, and that's great. It means that you've done exactly what I'd hoped: you've looked deep within yourself and found your passion, your true path, the reason you've been put on this earth. You're ready to stop letting your past determine your future. You've already begun to move forward.

Cherish Your Friends and Loved Ones

Now that you've gathered your supportive friends and loved ones about you, make sure that you're there to support them. Take every opportunity to let them know how much they mean to you and how much they enrich your life. You've been granted these gifts; just make sure you don't take them for granted. Little things mean a lot. Make a phone call to say I miss you and I love you. How are you? Is there anything I can do for you today? Remember and acknowledge important occasions in their lives—birthdays, anniversaries, graduations, and so on. Make time for them; it will be time well spent. By nourishing relationships with your soul mates you'll be nourishing yourself.

If you're committed to finding a life mate who is also a soul mate, get up off your couch and do something about it. What are the qualities you hope to find in a soul mate? Keep your eyes, ears, and above all your heart open so that you recognize him or her when your paths cross. Soul mates are likely to appear in your life in unexpected places, so you have to be there and be aware.

Keep the Energy of Your Living Space Positive and Productive

Once you've banished any lingering negativity from your living space and performed some psychic feng shui to get the positive energy flowing freely, you'll need to be sure that your environment continues to support your goals.

Take care of your home and your work space and they will take care of you. If you begin to find yourself feeling angry, depressed, or uncomfortable in places where you should feel serene, go back and do one of the cleansing rituals we discussed in the chapter on key #3. Review the meanings of the feng shui colors and elements and see if there's something more you can do to "accentuate the positive, eliminate the negative," as the old song goes. And keep up with all the negative stuff that can accumulate very quickly when we're busy doing other things. Remember: the more positive your environment, the better you'll be able to accomplish all the other important things you want to do in your life.

Step into Your Power to Enhance Your Prosperity

You now understand that you have the power to bring whatever your heart desires into your life. You've allowed yourself to visualize yourself having followed your passions and achieved your goals. You've committed yourself totally to the process. What this means is that you have all the tools you need to do whatever you want.

The only thing that can hold you back now is yourself. You've made a plan, you know where you're starting from, and you know where you're going and how you intend to get there. Now you just need to take the first steps, continue to put one foot in front of the other, and you will reach your destination. You may run into roadblocks and have to take a detour or two; that's to be expected. But with your newfound intention clear in your mind, you'll be able to stay positive and do whatever it takes to keep moving forward. If you ever find that doubts are creeping in, go back to key #4 and do the visualization on pages 140 to 142, reaffirming to yourself your positive intention to make it happen. With that intention firmly in mind you'll be ready to step into your greatness.

Continue to Develop Your Spiritual Strength

As you continue to make positive changes in your life, there will, no doubt, be moments when you feel a little scared. Change, as I've said, can be scary. The most powerful thing you can do to increase your sense of safety is to strengthen your inborn spirituality.

However you personally relate to the higher power, it is your belief that you are being guided by a purpose greater than yourself that will allow you to have continued faith and hope for the future. However, it's worth repeating here that having faith in a higher power does not mean abdicating responsibility for the decisions you make for yourself or blaming some invisible superior being for the bad things that may happen in your life. Rather, having faith in a higher power means that you'll be able to make peace with the fact that whatever comes into your life happens for a reason, however good or bad it might seem at the time. In fact, keeping your faith during times of adversity is one of the most powerful ways to increase your spiritual strength. Continue to use meditation, prayer, and journaling to increase your own spiritual strength and connect with the higher power. Keep your heart and mind open so that, when you ask for a sign, you are ready to receive it.

Continue to Nurture Your Emotional and Physical Well-being

Just because taking care of your physical and emotional self was the last key we talked about for unlocking your life's treasures, that doesn't mean it's last in terms of importance. In fact, all the keys I've provided in this book are equally important, and if you don't look after your own well-being you'll find it much more difficult to make the best use of your other treasures.

I've provided a few powerful tips you can use for making sure you take care of yourself, but in truth, all the strategies and exercises throughout the entire book will work together to enrich all aspects of yourself on every level. I urge you to use them all in good health.

Use All Your Treasures to Create a Structure for Your Life

My goal throughout this process has been to provide you with a variety of tools you can use together to create a positive structure for your life. When you invest your money wisely, you will create a portfolio that continues to multiply and strengthen your monetary base. The same is true when you're investing in yourself. Consider the six keys in this book the stocks and bonds of your personal investment package. The more they work together to enhance and balance one another, the more your internal power and wealth will increase. When you're operating from a strong base, there's no wind that can knock you off course, no weight you can't lift from your shoulders.